THE
FOURTH
DIMENSION

by

DR. PAUL YONGGI CHO

LOGOS INTERNATIONAL
Plainfield, New Jersey

DEDICATION

This book is dedicated to the many...

...seeking...

...searching...

...and struggling...

to find and walk a consistent road of faith in their Christian lives.

THE FOURTH DIMENSION
Copyright © 1979 by Paul Yonggi Cho
All rights reserved
Printed in the United States of America
Library of Congress Catalog Card Number: 79-65588
International Standard Book Number: 0-88270-380-3
Logos International, Plainfield, New Jersey 07060

FOREWORD

I count it a great honor to write these words as a foreword to this exciting book by my brother in Christ, Paul Yonggi Cho. I am personally indebted to him for spiritual strength, and for insights I have received from God through this great Christian pastor.

I was ministering to his huge congregation in Seoul, Korea, when we received a telephone call that our daughter was tragically injured in a horrible traffic accident in Iowa. Accompanying us to the plane as my wife and I left in haste was our dear friend, Paul Yonggi Cho, prayerfully supporting and sustaining us. And when I arrived some hours later to sit through the black night hours at the pain-wracked side of my daughter, whose left leg had just been amputated and whose life had just been snatched from death, I found myself reading page after page of the unpublished manuscript of this book for which I now, with enthusiasm, offer a word or two.

I discovered the reality of that dynamic dimension in prayer that comes through visualizing the healing experience. Line after line, of the original manuscript, was underlined by this travel-weary pastor, this suffering father. I can only hope and pray that many

Christians—and unbelievers too!—will find this book coming into their hands and drawing from it the amazing spiritual truths that its pages contain.

Don't try to understand it. Just start to enjoy it! It's true. It works. I tried it. Thank you—Paul Yonggi Cho—for allowing the Holy Spirit to give this message to us and to the world. God loves you and so do I!

Robert H. Schuller

TABLE OF CONTENTS

Suggested Reading

Other books on church growth

New!
Cells for Life Positive, how-to guidance for stimulating growth among home fellowships, cell groups and churches interested in "share and care" gatherings in homes.

Miracle in Darien Bob Slosser's account of a church's experiment in faith: allowing Christ to be the true head of their church.

The Holy Spirit and You A comprehensive, informal teaching on the baptism and gifts of the Holy Spirit. By the author of *Nine O'Clock in the Morning*.

The Exploding Church The story of Tommy Reid's spiritual growth and the development of his ministry. A challenge to clergy and lay people to see their churches grow in commitment, unity and love.

Your Pastor, Your Shepherd The veteran pastor of a large Detroit church tackles the subject of shepherding and addresses the controversial questions of authority, discipline, tithing, home fellowships and personal ministry.

Available at your local bookstore
Or from the publisher

Logos International
201 Church Street
Plainfield, New Jersey 07060

PREFACE

Life Full And Free

In the chaos that followed the Korean Conflict, I was among the many struggling for existence. Poor but persistent, I held several jobs in the course of a single day.

One afternoon I was working as a tutor. Suddenly I felt something oozing up from deep inside my chest. My mouth felt full. I thought I would choke.

As I opened my mouth, blood began to gush out. I tried to stop the bleeding, but blood continued to flow from my nostrils and mouth. My stomach and chest soon filled with blood. Severely weakened, I fainted.

When I returned to consciousness everything seemed to be spinning. Shaken, I barely managed to travel home.

I was nineteen years old. And I was dying.

Go Home, Young Man

Frightened, my parents immediately sold enough of their possessions to take me to a famous hospital for treatment. The doctor's examinations were careful, their diagnosis: incurable tuberculosis.

When I heard their assessment, I realized how badly I

wanted to live. My desires for the future were to end before I even had the chance to start fully living.

Desperate, I turned to the physician who had pronounced the grim diagnosis. "Doctor," I plead, "isn't there anything you can do for me?"

His reply was to resound often in my mind. "No. This type of tuberculosis is very unusual. It is spreading so fast that there is no way to arrest it.

"You have three, at the most four, months to live. Go home, young man. Eat anything you want. Say good-bye to your friends."

Dejected, I left the hospital. I passed hundreds of refugees on the streets, and felt a kindred spirit. Feeling totally alone, I was one of the hopeless.

I returned home in a dazed condition. Ready to die, I hung a three month calendar on the wall. Raised a Buddhist, I prayed daily that Buddha would help me. But no hope came, and I grew continually worse.

Sensing that my time to live was shortening, I gave up faith in Buddha. It was then that I began to cry to the unknown God. Little did I know how great an impact His response would have on my life.

Touching Tears

A few days later a high school girl visited me, and began to talk about Jesus Christ. She told me about Christ's virgin birth, His death on a cross, His resurrection, and salvation through grace. These stories seemed nonsense to me. I neither accepted her stories, nor paid much attention to this ignorant young female. Her departure left me with one emotion: relief.

But the next day she returned. She came again and again, every time troubling me with stories about the God-man, Jesus. After more than a week of these visits, I became greatly agitated, and roughly rebuked her.

She did not run away in shame, nor retaliate in anger. She simply knelt down, and began to pray for me. Large tears rolled down her cheeks, reflecting a compassion foreign to my well-organized and sterile Buddhist philosophies and rituals.

When I saw her tears, my heart was deeply touched. There was something different in this young girl. She was not reciting religious stories to me; she was living what she believed. Through her love and tears I could feel the presence of God.

"Young lady," I entreated, "please don't cry. I am sorry. I now know about your Christian love. Since I am dying I will become a Christian for you."

Her response was immediate. Her face brightened into a glow, and she praised God. Shaking hands with me, she gave me her Bible.

"Search the Bible," she instructed. "If you read it faithfully you will find the words of life."

That was the first time in my life I had ever held a Bible. Constantly struggling to gasp air into my lungs, I opened to the Book of Genesis.

Turning the pages to Matthew, she smiled: "Sir, you are so sick that if you start from Genesis, I don't think you will last long enough to finish Revelation. If you start from the Book of Matthew, you will have enough time."

Expecting to find deep moral and philosophical religious teachings, I was shocked at what I read. "Abraham begat Isaac; Isaac begat Jacob; and Jacob begat Judas and his brethren."

I felt very foolish. I closed the Bible saying, "Young lady, I won't read this Bible. This is only a story of one man begetting another. I would rather read a telephone directory."

"Sir, she replied. "You don't recognize these names right now. But as you read on, these names will come to hold special meaning for you." Encouraged, I began reading the Bible again.

The Living Lord

As I read I did not find any systematized philosophies, any theories of medical science, or any religious rituals. But I did find one striking theme: The Bible constantly talked about Jesus Christ, the Son of God.

The imminence of my death had brought me to the realization that I needed something greater than a religion, greater than a philosophy, and even greater than sympathy for the trials of human existence. I needed someone who could share my struggles and sufferings, someone who could give me victory.

Through reading the Bible I discovered that someone to be the Lord Jesus Christ:

The Person Jesus Christ was not bringing a religion, a code of ethics, nor a series of rituals. In a profoundly practical way, Jesus was bringing salvation to humanity. Hating sin, Christ loved the sinner, accepting all who came to Him. Deeply aware of my sins, I knew I needed His forgiveness.

Christ healed the sick. The ill and infirm came to Him, and He healed all He touched. This put faith in my heart. I became hopeful that He might heal me, too.

Christ gave peace to the troubled. He urged, "Have faith in God! Don't be troubled! There is no reason to fear!" Christ hated fear, showing man that he was born to live by faith. Christ gave confidence, faith and peace to those who came to receive help. This tremendous message thrilled my heart.

Christ raised the dead. I never found one incident in the Bible where Christ conducted a funeral service. He brought the dead to life, changing funeral services into magnificent resurrections.

Most outstanding in my mind was Christ's mercy to the demon possessed. During the Korean War many people lost their families and businesses. Suffering from nervous breakdowns, many became completely possessed by the devil. Bereft of shelter, they wandered aimlessly around the streets.

Christ was even ready to meet this challenge. He cast out demons and restored the possessed to a life of normalcy. Christ's love was powerful, touching the lives and needs of all who came to Him.

Convinced that Jesus Christ was alive and moved by the vitality of His ministry, I knelt down. I asked Christ to come into my heart, to save, heal and deliver me from death.

Instantly the joy of salvation and the peace of Christ's forgiveness surged over me. I knew that I was saved. Filled with the Holy Spirit, I stood up and shouted, "Glory be to the Lord!"

From that time on I read the Bible like a starving man eats bread. The Bible supplied foundation for all the faith I needed. Despite the prognosis and old feelings of fear, I soon knew I was going to live. Instead of dying in three months, I was out of my deathbed in six.

Since that time I had been preaching the dynamic Gospel of Jesus Christ. The girl whose name I never knew taught me the most precious name I will ever know.

Through the years God has helped me to understand several important principles of faith. These are the principles I share with you in the chapters that follow, in order that you can enter a deeper dimension and more abundant life.

Christ is unchanging. He is the same yesterday, today and forever.

Christ wants to bear your burdens. Jesus can forgive and heal you. He can cast out satan, and give you confidence, faith and peace.

Christ wants to give you life eternal and be a present part of your daily living. While thieves come to kill and destroy, Jesus Christ comes to give you life, life full and free.

Through the presence of the Holy Spirit, Jesus is with you right now. Christ desires to heal you, and to deliver you from death. He is your living Lord. Put your faith in Jesus Christ, and expect a miracle today.

1

INCUBATION: A LAW OF FAITH

God will never bring about any of His great works without coming through your own personal faith. It is taken for granted that you do have faith, for the Bible says that God has dealt to each and every one of us a measure of faith. You have faith whether you feel it or not. You may try to feel faith, but when you need faith, then faith is there. It is there for your use, like having two arms; when you need to use them, you just reach out your arms and move them. I do not need to feel that my two arms are hanging on my shoulders to know that I have them.

There are, however, certain ways your faith works, and links you to the Heavenly Father who dwells within you. The Bible says that faith is the substance of things hoped for, a substance which first has a stage of development—of incubation—before its usage can be full and effective. You might now ask, "What are the elements needed to make my faith usable?" There are four basic steps to the process of incubation.

Envision a Clear-cut Objective

First, to use your faith you must be able to envision a clear-cut objective. Faith is the substance of things, clear-cut things, hoped for. If you have only a vague idea about your goal, then you are out of touch with the One who could answer your prayer. You must have a clear and defined faith goal. I learned this lesson in a very peculiar situation.

I had been in the ministry for quite a few months, and was so poverty-stricken that, as far as material things are concerned, I had nothing. I was not married, and was living in one small room. I had no desk, no chair, and no bed and was eating on the floor, sleeping on the floor and studying on the floor, but walking miles and miles everyday to carry out soul winning.

But one day while reading my Bible, I was tremendously impressed by God's promises. The Bible said that if I would just put my faith in Jesus, praying in His name, that I would receive everything. The Bible also taught me that I was the son of God, a child of the King of kings, and of the Lord of lords!

So I said, "Father! Why should a child of the King of kings, and of the Lord of lords, live without a desk, chair and bed, and walk mile after mile everyday? At least I should have a humble desk and chair to sit on, and a humble bicycle to ride on to do my home visitation." I felt that according to Scripture I could ask for these kinds of things from the Lord. I knelt down and prayed, "Father, now I am praying. Please send me a desk, chair and bicycle." I believed and praised God.

From that moment on I was waiting for the delivery of each thing I had prayed for. A month passed with no answer. Then two months, three, four, five, six, and still I was waiting; but nothing happened. Then one rainy day I was really depressed, and not having any food by that evening was so hungry, tired and depressed I started complaining, "Lord, I asked you to supply me with a desk, a chair, and a bicycle several months ago, but you have not supplied me with any of those things. Now you see me as I am here preaching the Gospel to the poverty stricken people of this slum area. How can I ask them to exercise faith when I cannot even practice it myself? How can I ask them to put their faith in the Lord, and truly live by the Word, and not by bread?

"My Father! I am very discouraged. I am not sure about this, but I do know I cannot deny the Word of God. The Word must stand, and I am sure that you are going to answer me, but this time I'm just not sure when or how. If you are going to answer my prayer after my death, what kind of profit will that have for me? If you are ever going to answer my prayer, please speed it up. Please!"

Then I sat down and began to cry. Suddenly I felt a serenity, and a feeling of tranquility came into my soul. Whenever I have that kind of feeling, a sense of the presence of God, He always speaks; so I waited. Then that still, small voice welled up in my soul, and the Spirit said, "My son, I heard your prayer a long time ago."

Right away I blurted out, "Then where are my desk, chair and bicycle?"

The Spirit then said, "Yes, that is the trouble with you, and with all my children. They beg me, demanding every kind of request, but they ask in such vague terms that I can't answer. Don't you know that there are dozens of kinds of desks, chairs and bicycles? But you've simply asked me for a desk, chair and bicycle. You never ordered a specific desk, chair or bicycle."

That was a turning point in my life. No professor in the Bible college ever taught me along these lines. I had made a mistake, and it was an eyeopener for me.

I then said, "Lord, do you really want me to pray in definite terms?" This time the Lord led me to turn to Hebrews, the eleventh chapter: "Faith is the substance of things," clear-cut things, "hoped for."

I knelt down again and said, "Father, I'm sorry. I made a great mistake, and I misunderstood you. I cancel all my past prayers. I'll start all over again."

So I gave the size of the desk, which was to be made of Philippine mahogany. I wanted the best kind of chair, one made with an iron frame, and with rollers on the tips, so that when I sat on it I could push myself around like a big shot.

Then I came to the bicycle, and I really gave much consideration to the matter, because there were so many kinds of bicycles: Korean, Japanese, Formosan, German. But in those days bicycles made in Korea or Japan were usually quite flimsy. I wanted to have a very strong, sturdy bicycle; and since any machine made in the U.S. was the best, I said, "Father, I want to have a bicycle made in the U.S.A., with gears on the side so that I can even regulate speed." I ordered these things in such articulate terms that God could not make a mistake in delivering them. Then I felt faith flowing up and out of my heart, and I was rejoicing in the Lord; that night I slept like a baby.

But when I awoke at 4:30 the next morning to prepare for the early morning prayer meeting, I suddenly found that my heart was empty. The evening before, I had all the faith in the world, but while I slept faith took wing and left me. I could not feel anything in my heart. I said, "Father, this is terrible. It is one thing to have faith, but it's entirely different to keep that faith till I receive your answer."

This is a trouble common to all Christians. They have a special guest speaker, and are filled with faith when he ministers to them, but before they reach their homes they have lost it all. Their faith takes wing and flies away.

On that morning while I was reading the Bible, and looking for a particular scripture to speak on, suddenly my eyes fell upon Romans 4:17, "God raises the dead, and calls those things which be not as if they were." My heart fastened to that scripture, and it began to boil in my heart. I said to myself, "I might as well just call those things which are not as if they were, as if I already had them." I had received the answer to the problem of how to keep one's faith.

I rushed out to our tent church where the people had already begun praying, and after a few songs I started preaching. I expounded that scripture, and then said, "Folks, by the blessings of God I have a desk made of Philippine mahogany, a beautiful chair with an iron frame and rollers on the tips, and a bicycle made in the U.S.A. with gears on the side. Praise God! I've received all these things."

The people just gasped, because they knew that I was absolutely poverty stricken. I was bragging about these things, and they could not believe their ears. In faith I was really praising God, doing just as the Word of God told me to do.

After the service, as I was walking out, three young fellows followed me and said, "Pastor, we want to see those things."

I was taken aback and frightened, because I had not counted on having to show any of those things. These people were living in a slum area, and once they knew I had lied, it would be my last time to minister there. They would never come back. I was in a terrible situation, so I began to pray to the Lord, "Lord, from the beginning this wasn't my idea. It was your idea for me to tell it like that. I just obeyed you, and now I'm in a terrible situation. I said it as if I had it, and now how can I explain this? You've got to always help me."

Then the Lord came and helped me, and an idea floated up from my heart. I said, "You come over to my room and see."

They all came, and they looked around to find the bicycle, chair and desk. I said, "Don't look around. I'll show you later."

I pointed my finger at Mr. Park, who is now pastor of one of the largest Assemblies of God churches in Korea, and said, "I'll ask you a few questions. If you can answer my questions, I'll show you all of those things. How long were you in your mother's womb before you were born into this world?"

He scratched his head and said, "Well, nine months."

I then replied, "What were you doing for nine months in your mother's womb?"

"Oh, I was growing."

"But," I said, "no one saw you."

"No one could see me because I was inside of my mother."

Then I said, "You were as much a baby inside your mother's womb as you were when you were born into the world. You gave me the right answer. Last evening I knelt down here and prayed to the Lord for that desk, chair and bicycle, and by the power of the Holy Spirit, I conceived that desk, chair and bicycle. It is as if they're inside me, growing right now. And they are as much a desk, chair and bicycle as when they will be seen by people at the time of their delivery."

They started laughing and laughing. They said, "This is the first time we've ever seen a man pregnant with a bicycle, chair and desk." Rushing out of my room they began to spread the rumour all over town that the minister was pregnant with a bicycle, chair and desk. I could hardly walk through that town because women would gather to look at me and giggle. Mischievous youngsters would come to me on Sunday, touch my stomach and say, "Pastor, how big you are becoming!"

But all those days I knew that I had every one of those things growing in me. It just takes time, as a mother takes time to give birth to a child. It takes time

for you, too, because you become pregnant with all of
your clear-cut objectives.

I was praising the Lord, and sure enough, when the
time came, I had every one of those things. I had exactly
all the things I had asked for–a desk made out of
Philippine mahogany; a chair made by the Japanese
Mitsubishi Company, with rollers on the tips so that
I could roll around when I sat on it; and a slightly
used bicycle, with gears on the side, from an American
missionary's son. I brought that desk, chair and bicycle
into my house and was completely changed in my
prayer attitude.

Until that time I had always prayed in vague
terms, but from that time until now I have never prayed
in vague terms. If God were ever to answer your vague
prayers, then you would never recognize that prayer as
being answered by God. You must ask definitely and
specifically.

The Lord never welcomes vague prayers. When the
son of Timaeus, the blind Bartimaeus, came running
after Jesus Christ, he cried, "Oh, thou Son of David, be
merciful to me." Although everybody knew that Bartimaeus was asking for the healing of his blindness,
Christ asked, "What do you want me to do for you?"
Christ wants very specific requests. Bartimaeus said,
"Sir, I want to see." Jesus replied, "It shall be done

unto you as you believe." Bartimaeus opened his eyes.

But before he asked specifically for the healing of his blindness, Christ never pronounced the healing. When you bring your request to the Lord, come with a specific request, with a definite objective, with a clear-cut goal.

Once when I was the visiting preacher in a church, the pastor's wife invited me to the pastor's office. The pastor asked, "Cho, would you please pray for a lady here?"

I asked, "For what?"

"Well, she wants to get married, and she still hasn't found a husband."

"Ask her to come in."

So in she walked, a nice spinster over thirty years old. I asked her, "Sister, how long have you been praying for a husband?"

She answered, "For more than ten years."

"Why hasn't God answered your prayer for these more than ten years?" I asked. "What kind of husband have you been asking for?"

She shrugged her shoulders, "Well, that's up to God. God knows all."

"That's your mistake. God never works by Himself, but only through you. God is the eternal source, but He only works through your requests. Do you really want me to pray for you?"

"Yes."

"Okay, bring me some white paper and a pencil, and sit down in front of me." She sat down and I said, "If you write down the answers to my questions, then I'll pray for you. Number one: now, you really want a husband, but what kind of husband do you want— Asian, Caucasian, or Black?"

"Caucasian."

"Okay. Write it down. Number two: do you want your husband to be as tall as six feet, or as small as five feet?"

"Oh, I want to have a tall husband."

"Write that down. Number three: do you want your husband to be slim and nice looking, or just pleasantly plump?"

"I want to have him skinny."

"Write down *skinny*. Number four: what kind of hobby do you want your husband to have?"

"Well, musical."

"Okay, write down *musical*. Number five: what kind of job do you want your husband to have?"

"Schoolteacher."

"Okay. Write down *schoolteacher*," I went through ten points with her, and then said, "Please read aloud your list." So she read each point, 1 through 10, with a loud voice. Then I said, "Close your eyes. Can you see your husband now?"

"Yes, I can see him clearly."

"Okay. Let's order him now. Until you see your husband clearly in your imagination you can't order, because God will never answer. You must see him clearly before you begin to pray. God never answers vague prayers."

So she knelt down and I laid my hands on her, "Oh, God, now she knows her husband. I see her husband. You know her husband. We order him in the name of Jesus Christ."

"Sister, take this written paper to your home and paste it on a mirror. Every evening before you go to sleep read those ten points aloud, and every morning when you get up read those ten points aloud, and praise God for the answer."

One year passed, and I was passing through that area again when the wife of the minister called me on the telephone. She said, "Pastor, would you come and have lunch with us?"

"Of course I will," so I went to eat lunch.

As soon as I arrived at the cafeteria she said, "Oh, she got married! She got married!"

"Who got married?"

"Do you remember that girl you prayed for? You

asked her to write down those ten points? She got married!"

"Yes, now I remember. What happened?"

"That particular summer at the church one high school music teacher came in with a quartet, staying in that church for a week to carry out a singing revival. He was a single man, and all of the young girls were crazy about him; they wanted to date him, but this guy was nonchalant to the young girls. Yet he was fascinated with this older spinster. He was always hanging around her, and before he left he asked her to marry him. Eventually she not so reluctantly gave her consent.

They were happily married in that church, and on their marriage day her mother took that paper written with the ten points, and read it publicly before the people, then tore it up."

It sounds like a story, but it really works like that. I want to remind you of one thing: God is within you. God never works anything independently of you that concerns your life. God is only going to work through your thinking, through your beliefs; so, whenever you want to receive answers from the Lord, bring out that clear-cut objective.

Do not say, "Oh, God, bless me, bless me!" Do you know how many blessings the Bible has? Over 8,000 promises. If you say, "Oh God, bless me," then God might ask you, "What kind of blessing out of over 8,000 promises do you want?" So be very definite. Take out your notebook, write it down, see it clearly.

I always ask God to give a revival to my church according to a definite number. In 1960 I began to pray, "God, give us one thousand more members each year." And until 1969, one thousand members were added to my church every year.

But in 1969 I changed my mind and thought, "If God could give one thousand members per year, why shouldn't I ask God to give one thousand members per month?" So since 1970 I started praying, "Father, give us one thousand members per month."

At first God gave 600, then He began to give more than 1,000 per month. Last year we received more than 12,000 members in our church. I lifted my goal higher this year, and we are now going to have 15,000 additional members; next year I can easily ask for 20,000. If you have a definite request, and if you really see it, then you can have it.

When I was building the present church structure, which seats 10,000, even before they poured the concrete, I saw it clearly in my imagination. I walked hundreds of times in that building, and I felt the magnificent presence of the Holy Spirit there. I felt the magnitude of that church, a thrill to my heart. You must see your objective so vividly and graphically that you can really feel it in your emotions. If you do not exercise this law of faith you can never really get an answer to everything you request.

Now in my prayers I always try to see clearly. I want to see my objective so vividly that I feel a thrill in my heart. It is then that this first condition is completed.

Have A Burning Desire

Secondly, if you have a vivid picture, you should have a burning desire for those objectives. Many people just pray casually, "God, answer my prayer." and before walking out of the church have forgotten all the things they prayed for. That kind of attitude will never bring the faith and touch of God. You need to have a burning desire.

Proverbs 10:24 reads, "The desire of the righteous shall be granted." Psalms 37:4 says, "Delight thyself also in the Lord; and He shall give thee the desires of thine heart." You should have a burning desire for a goal, and you must keep on seeing that goal accomplished.

When I started my ministry in 1958 I had a burning desire in my soul, a burning goal to build the largest church in Korea. That desire was burning in me so much that I was living with it, sleeping with it, and walking with it. Now after twenty years it has been said that my church is the largest church in the world.

You have to have a burning desire in your heart. If you do not have a burning desire, then wait and ask God to impart His desire to your heart. God does not like the lukewarm, for He specializes only in the red-hot; if you have that red-hot burning desire, then you are going to have results.

Pray for Assurance

Third, you must have the substance, or assurance. "Substance" in the Greek language is *hupostasis*. In the English language this can be translated "title deed, or legal paper." When you have a clear goal, and you have this desire burning in your heart to a boiling point, then you should kneel down and pray until you receive the substance, the assurance.

When I was conducting a meeting in Hawaii, one Japanese woman came and asked me how long she should pray to receive assurance. I told her that sometimes it takes only a minute, and if she would have peace and assurance in her heart in that instant, she would not need to pray any longer. "But," I told her, "it could sometimes take two minutes, two hours, two weeks, two months, or two years; but whatever the length of time, you should pray through until you have this substance."

Westerners are often wrapped up in the problem of trying to live according to schedules. Everything is rush, rush, rush. Soon they start losing the time to have fellowship with family and friends, and even the time to wait upon the Lord. Everything seems instant: instant breakfast, T.V. dinners, fast food counters—all is ready in five minutes. So when going to church they seem to pray, "Oh, God, answer me. I have no time— five minutes—and if you don't answer me quickly, forget about it." They are not waiting upon the Lord.

Americans have often turned churches into a place for lengthy entertainment. In Korea we have gotten rid of all that entertainment. We make our announcements very short, with the Word of God taking preeminence. After preaching the Word of God we have two or three specials—then we conclude. But the Word of God is always uppermost.

I had been invited to speak in an evening service at a church in Alabama. The service opened at seven o'clock, and the announcements and musical preliminaries took almost two hours; I got sleepy just sitting there. The people also began to feel tired, and the preacher came to me and said, "Cho, please speak only ten minutes tonight. We have a wonderful television program coming on tonight, so I want you to preach for only ten minutes." I had come all the way from Korea, by his invitation, to speak ten minutes that evening.

In such a church you cannot have the Lord's full blessings. In a church there needs to be a long time of waiting upon the Lord, and of praising Him, as well as a solid preaching of the Word of God; that builds faith. And you must wait upon the Lord until you get the assurance.

When we needed five million dollars to build the church already contracted, I had a clear-cut vision, a clear-cut goal, and a burning desire to build this church which would seat 10,000 people. But my heart was full of fear. I was shaky, fearful, and I had no assurance. I was like a frightened rabbit, and that five million dollars looked like Mount Everest. To rich foreigners a million dollars may mean relatively little; but to Koreans a million dollars means a great deal of money. So I began to pray like a person dying. I said, "Lord, now they've started working. But still I have no assurance. I don't know where we can get all this money."

I began travailing. A month passed, and still I had no peace and no assurance. A second month passed and I was praying into the middle of the nights. I would roll out of the bed and go to the corner and cry, sobbing my heart out. My wife thought that I was losing my mind, but I was mentally blinded. I would just stand, without thinking, worrying about the five million dollars.

After I prayed incessantly like that for three months, one morning my wife called, "Honey, breakfast is ready." As I was walking out of my study, just about to sit in the chair, suddenly the heavens opened up and the tremendous blessings of the Lord poured into my heart! And this great title deed, the substance and the assurance, were imparted into my soul. Suddenly I jumped out of my chair like a shot and I began to shout, "I've got it, I've got it, oh, I've got it!!"

My wife rushed out of the kitchen and when I looked at her I saw that her face was absolutely pale. She was frightened, and taking me, said, "Honey, what's happened to you? Are you all right? Sit down."

"I've got it!" I replied.

"What do you have?"

"I have five million dollars," I strongly asserted.

Then she said, "You are really crazy now. Really crazy."

"But Honey, I've got all these five million dollars inside of me. They're growing now! Oh, inside me it's growing!!" Suddenly those five million dollars had turned into a small pebble on my palm. I prayed with assurance. My faith reached out, and I grabbed hold of that five million dollars; it was mine.

I got the substance, and once you have the substance—the title deed, the legal paper—whether you see those things or not, legally those things are bound to come to you because legally those things belong to you. So pray through until you have this assurance.

I prayed through the early part of this year and God gave me the assurance of a total of 50,000 members in my church. So I claimed it, and in my heart I see 50,000 members. Those members are inside of me, growing, and as the vision grows inside of me, the same is growing outside. This is the secret: pray until you get the substance, the assurance.

Speak the Word

Fourth, you should show evidence of your faith. The Bible says God raised the dead. That means that God performed miracles, calling "those things which be not as if they were."

Abraham was one hundred years old, and Sarah was ninety. They had a clear-cut goal—to have a son. They had a burning desire to have this son, and they prayed for twenty-five years. Eventually God gave them a promise, and when they received the assurance, God immediately changed their names: "You are no more Abram, but Abraham, the father of many nations; and you should not call your wife Sara, but Sarah, the princess."

Abraham protested to God, "Father, people will laugh at us. We don't even have a puppy in our home, and you mean you want us to change our names to 'father of many nations,' and 'princess'? My, all the people in town will call us crazy!"

But God might have said, "If you ever want to work with me you should do as I do. I call those things which be not as if they were, and if you don't speak boldly as if you already had what now is not, then you are out of my category."

So Abraham changed his name. He came to his wife and said, "Wife, now my name is changed. I am no more Abram, but Abraham, 'the father of many nations,' for God changed my name. Your name is no more Sara; but Sarah."

Evening came and Abraham was walking far down in the valley. Sarah prepared a meal and she called to her husband, "Abraham! The supper is ready," those phrases reverberating throughout all of the village.

The village people stopped working. They probably said, "Listen! She is calling her husband Abraham, 'the father of many nations!' Oh, poor Sarah! She wanted to have a child so badly in her ninetieth year that she's started calling her husband 'the father of many nations!' She's lost her mind. Oh, we feel sorry for her."

Then suddenly they heard a big baritone sound from the valley. "Sarah, I'm coming."

"What?!" they probably murmured, "Sarah, 'the princess, the mother of many children?' Oh, he's in the same boat! They're crazy together."

But Abraham and Sarah ignored the criticism of the villagers. They talked back to each other: "the father of many nations," and "the princess." And exactly as they called each other, exactly as they gave affirmation, they had a beautiful child, Isaac, meaning "smile."

Brothers and sisters, do you like to see a smile? Do you like smiles in your home? Do you like to have a smile in your businesses and churches? Use the law of faith! Then you can see the birth of Isaac again and again in your life.

Miracles come not by blindly struggling. There are laws in the spiritual realm, and you have endless resources in your heart. God is dwelling within you; but God is not going to do anything for you without coming through your own life. God is going to co-operate with you to accomplish great things. God is the same, for Jehovah never changes; but before a person changes, God cannot manifest himself to them. God used Moses and Joshua, and other men of giant faith; but when they passed away and people began to backslide, God stopped manifesting His power.

God wants to manifest Himself through you today, just as He manifested Himself through Christ 2,000 years ago. He is just as powerful as He was before, and He is depending upon you. I claim that I could build a church which has more than 10,000 members very easily in the States, as well as in Germany or in Tokyo, for the vision for a church is not built in the external world, but inside a man or woman.

What becomes pregnant in your heart and mind is going to come out in your circumstance. Watch your heart and your mind more than anything else. Do not try to find the answer of God through another person, for God's answer comes to your spirit, and through your spirit the answer comes to your circumstances.

Claim and speak the word of assurance, for your word actually goes out and creates. God spoke and the whole world came into being. Your word is the material which the Holy Spirit uses to create.

So give the word, for this is very important. The church today has lost the art of giving commands. We Christians are becoming perennial beggars, for constantly we are begging. On the bank of the Red Sea Moses begged, "Oh God, help us! The Egyptians are coming." God rebuked him saying, "Moses, why are you crying to me? Give the command and the Red

Sea shall be divided.'"

There are times for you to pray, but there are also times for you to give the command. You must pray through in your prayer closet, but when you come out to the battlefield, you are coming to give the word of creation. When you read the life of Jesus Christ you see that He always gave the command. He prayed all night, but when He came out to the front lines He commanded that the people be healed. He commanded the sea to be calm. He commanded the devil to leave.

And His disciples did exactly the same thing. To the beggar Peter commanded, "Silver and gold have I none, but what I have, give I unto you. Rise up in the name of Jesus Christ!" To the body of a dead woman Peter commanded, "Dorcas, rise up!" To the cripple at Lystra Paul commanded, "Stand on your feet!" He gave the word of creation.

The Bible says to heal the sick. In James the Bible says, "The prayer of faith shall save the sick." God clearly asks us to heal the sick; so in my church I heal the sick as the Holy Spirit guides me. I plainly stand before them and claim, "You are healed! Rise and stand up!" And I call the different healings out, and by the dozens and by the hundreds people have received healing.

A few months ago I was holding a meeting in a

Western country. One evening in the meeting we had about 1,500 people packed into this one place, and right in front of me was one lady in a wheelchair. She was so badly twisted that I felt depressed. I asked, "Lord, why did you put her in front of me? I can't exercise faith after seeing her." So I tried to avoid looking at her while I was preaching. I would look one way, and then suddenly turn around and look the other way; for the sight of her poured cold water on my heart.

At the close of the sermon the Holy Spirit suddenly spoke in my heart, "Walk down and lift her up."

I replied, "Dear Spirit, you really mean that I should go down and lift her up? She is so twisted, I wonder if Jesus Christ Himself could lift her up. I can't do it. I'm scared."

But the Holy Spirit said, "You go and lift her up."

I refused, saying, "Oh, no, I'm afraid."

So I started calling out the types of healing that the Holy Spirit showed me taking place in people other than this woman. First a blind lady was healed. She was so frightened when I called out her healing she shrieked and fainted, just after her eyes had suddenly opened. Then people began to be healed all over the auditorium. I kept calling out healings continuously but the Holy Spirit kept saying to me, "Go down and lift her up."

I replied, "Father, she is too twisted, and I'm scared."

In the last moments of the service I gave in, and when the pastor asked all the people to stand up and sing the concluding song, I slipped down and spoke with a whisper so people would not hear me. "Lady, if you wish, you could come out of that chair." Then I stood up and began to rush away.

When I turned around all the people had started shouting and clapping their hands, for that woman had stepped out of her wheelchair and started walking around the platform. I was foolish, for if I had lifted her up in the beginning I could have brought heaven down to that service; but I was scared.

Many people come and ask me whether I have the gift of faith, or the gift of healing. But I've searched through my heart and so far I have not found any gift in me. I believe that is because it is the Holy Spirit who has the gifts, all nine of them. He dwells within us, and within me. The Holy Spirit manifests Himself through me; I do not have any of the gifts, only the Holy Spirit, and I just obey Him, and believe in Him.

What kind of gift do I have? I will tell you the one gift I have—the gift of boldness. With this gift of boldness we just launch out by faith; then the Holy Spirit is going to follow after us. The Bible does not say that a sign shall go ahead of you; the Bible says that a sign shall follow you. You must go ahead so that the sign can follow you. Abide by the law of incubation, and throughout your life watch as sign after sign follows your path of faith.

You have the resources within you, and now you know the elements needed in incubation to make your faith usable. Get a clear-cut goal and objective. Have a desire that burns to the boiling point, then pray until you have the substance, the assurance. Then begin to speak the word about which you have been given assurance.

2

THE FOURTH DIMENSION

As there are certain steps that we must follow in order for our faith to be properly incubated, there is also a central truth concerning the nature of faith's realm that we need to understand. The most important lessons that I have learned about the nature of the realm of faith began as a result of what was at first an unpleasant experience.

In America ministers do not have this kind of problem, but in the Orient I have real trouble in preaching about the miraculous power of God, for in Buddhism monks also have performed fantastic miracles. Just recently in Korea one woman was dying from a case of terminal cancer, and no doctor could cure her. She went to many churches, then to a Buddhist monk. He took her to a grotto where many were praying, and she was completely healed and cleansed, and the cancer disappeared.

In Korea many people involved in yoga are healing the sick by yoga meditation. when attending meetings of the Japanese Sokagakkai, many are healed–some of stomach ulcers, the deaf and dumb hearing and speaking, and the blind seeing. So naturally we Christians, especially Pentecostal Christians, have real difficulty in explaining these occurrences. You cannot put these things away simply as a manifestation of the devil. But if the devil could do these things, why should not the Church of Jesus Christ do all the more?

I was quite troubled one day, for many of our Christians were not considering God's miracles to be of importance. They said, "Oh, how can we believe in God as an absolutely divine being? How can we call the Jehovah God the unique creator in heavenly places? We see miracles in Buddhism, miracles in yoga, and miracles in Sokagakkai. We see many miracles in the Oriental religions. Why should we claim Jehovah God as the only creator of the universe?"

But I knew that our God was the unique God, the only God, and the creator of the universe. So I made their questions a matter of prayer before God. I fasted and prayed, seeking the faith of the Lord, and His answers. Then a glorious revelation came to my heart, and I received a clear explanation. And from that time on I began to explain these things through my lectures in my church in Korea. Now I can give a satisfying reply to any of those questions, and I can easily give explanations, explanations as clear as a sunny day. Let me explain it to you.

The Four Dimensions

In the universe there are three types of spirits – the Holy Spirit of God, the spirit of the devil, and the human spirit. When you study geometry you put up two points, one here, and one there, and if you draw a line between the two you call it one dimension. It is just one line between the points, one dimension. But if you add line upon line by the hundreds of thousands, then one dimension naturally creates a second dimension, a plane. And if you stack up planes one upon another then it becomes cubic; this is called the third dimension. The material world and the whole earth belong to the third dimension.

This first dimension, a line, is contained in, and therefore controlled by, the second dimension, a plane; and the second dimension is included in, and therefore controlled by, the third dimension, the cube. Who then creates, contains, and controls the third dimension, the cubical world? You have the answer when you open the Bible and read in Genesis 1:2: "And the earth was without form, and void; and darkness was upon the face of the deep. And the Spirit of God moved upon the face of the waters."

But if you look into the original language of that scripture, it carries the meaning that the Spirit of the

Lord was incubating over the waters, brooding over the waters. This chaotic world belonged to the third dimension, but the Holy Spirit, who is pictured here incubating on the third dimension, belongs to the fourth dimension. So the spiritual kingdom of faith belongs to the fourth dimension.

Since the spiritual world hugged the third dimension, incubating on the third dimension, it was by this incubation of the fourth dimension on the third dimension that the earth was recreated. A new order was given out of the old, and life was given from death; beauty from ugliness; cleanliness from those things dirty; and abundance from poverty. Everything was created beautiful and wonderful by the incubation of the fourth dimension.

Then God spoke to my heart, "Son, as the second dimension includes and controls the first dimension, and the third dimension includes and controls the second dimension, so the fourth dimension includes and controls the third dimension, producing a creation of order and beauty. The spirit is the fourth dimension. Every human being is a spiritual being as well as a physical being. They have the fourth dimension as well as the third dimension in their hearts." So men, by exploring their spiritual sphere of the fourth dimension through the development of concentrated visions and dreams in their imaginations, can brood over and incubate the third dimension, influencing and changing it. This is what the Holy Spirit taught me.

So naturally these yoga people and Buddhist believers could explore and develop their human fourth dimension, their spiritual sphere; with clear-cut visions and mental pictures of health they could incubate over their bodies. By natural order the fourth dimension has power over the third dimension, and the human spirit, within limitations, has the power to give order and creation. God gave power to human beings to control the material world and to have dominion over material things, a responsibility they can carry out through the fourth dimension. Now unbelievers, by exploring and developing their inner spiritual being in such a way, can carry out dominion upon their third dimension, which includes their physical sicknesses and diseases.

Then the Holy Spirit said to me, "Look at the Sokagakkai. They belong to Satan; the human spirit joins up with the spirit of the evil fourth dimension, and with the evil fourth dimension they carry out dominion over their bodies and circumstances." The Holy Spirit showed me that it was in this manner that the magicians in Egypt carried out dominion over various occurrences, just as Moses did.

God then taught me that since we can link our spirit's fourth dimension to the fourth dimension of the Holy Father—the Creator of the universe—we can have all the more dominion over circumstances. Praise God! We can become fantastically creative, and we can exercise great control and power over the third dimension.

After receiving this revelation from the Lord I began to easily explain the happenings and miracles of other religions. People would come and challenge me, "We can do the same miracles."

I would say, "Yes, I know you can. It's because you have the fourth dimension in your spirit. You are developing your spirit and carrying out dominion over your body and circumstances. But that spirit is not a spirit with salvation, even though you can exercise those kinds of miracles.

"You are linked to the evil fourth dimension. The fourth dimension has the power to carry out dominion over the third dimension. You do have certain limited powers to carry out dominion over the third dimension, influencing your circumstances."

The Role of the Subconscious

In America I saw a lot of mind-expanding books, and I see similar things happening everywhere because of all this emphasis on the subconscious. What is the subconscious? The subconscious is your spirit. The Bible calls the subconscious the inner man, the man hidden in your heart.

Before psychology found the subconscious, Apostle Paul had already discovered it 2,000 years before, writing of the inner, hidden man. The Bible had that truth 2,000 years ago. Now scientists and psychologists make a great affair of this discovery, digging into the ideas of the subconscious and trying to direct its energies. Though the subconscious is in the fourth dimension, therefore having certain limited power, however, a great amount of deception is involved in what these people claim.

I was amazed coming to America and reading the books some American ministers gave me, for these books had almost made the subconscious into an almighty god, and that is a great deception. The subconscious has certain influence, but it is quite limited, and cannot create like our Almighty God can. I have begun to see in America the Unitarian Church try to develop the subconscious, the fourth dimension of the human spirit, and put that human spirit in the place of Jesus Christ; this indeed is great deception, and a great danger.

While we do recognize certain realities and truths

in these teachings, it is also important to realize that the devil occupies an evil fourth dimension. God, however, is holy, unique, and almighty. The fourth dimension is always creating and giving order, and carrying out dominion over the third dimension by the means of incubation. In Genesis the Spirit of the Lord was incubating, brooding over the water; He was like a hen sitting on her eggs, incubating them and hatching chickens. In much the same manner the Holy Spirit incubates the third dimension, so does the evil spirit incubate.

I was watching the television news in the U.S., and there was a great controversy in one area because a man was murdered, the lawyer claiming that this young murderer was intoxicated by violent television programs. There was a certain truth in that, for this boy, after watching television, began to exercise his fourth dimension. He was incubating on those acts of violence, and naturally he hatched the same sin.

The Language of the Fourth Dimension

My ministry has been revolutionized by discovering the truth of the fourth dimension, and you can revolutionize your life with it. You may wonder how we can incubate our subconscious. We dwell in limited bodies, whereas the Holy Spirit in His omnipresence can simply incubate over the whole earth. But we are so limited in space and time, and the only way for us to incubate is through our imaginations, through our visions and our dreams.

This is the reason the Holy Spirit comes to cooperate with us–to create, by helping young men to see visions, and old men to dream dreams. Through envisioning and dreaming dreams we can kick away the wall of limitations, and can stretch out to the universe. That is the reason that God's Word says, "Where there is no vision the people perish." If you have no vision, you are not being creative; and if you stop being creative, then you are going to perish.

Visions and dreams are the language of the fourth dimension, and the Holy Spirit communicates through them. Only through a vision and a dream can you visualize and dream bigger churches. You can visualize a new mission field; you can visualize the increase of your church. Through visualizing and dreaming you can incubate your future and hatch the results. Let me substantiate this with scriptural examples.

Do you know why Adam and Eve fell from grace? The devil knew that the fourth dimension visions and dreams in a person's mind could create a definite result. The devil used a tactic based on this premise; he invited Eve saying, "Eve, come over and look at that fruit on the forbidden tree. Looking at it is harmless, so why don't you come over and just look at it?"

So since simply looking at the fruit seemed to be harmless, Eve went and looked at the fruit of the tree. She looked at that tree not only once, but she kept looking. The Bible says in Genesis, the third chapter, verse six, "And when the woman saw that the tree was good for food...she took of the fruit thereof, and did eat." Before she partook she saw the tree, also seeing this fruit in her imagination. She played with the idea of eating the fruit, and brought that to her fourth dimension.

In the fourth dimension either good or evil is created. Eve brought that picture of the tree and fruit deep into her imagination, seeing the fruit clearly, imagining that it could make her as wise as God. Then she felt so attracted to that tree, it was as if she were being pulled toward it; next she took the fruit of the tree and ate, then gave some to her husband. And with that action, she fell.

If seeing is not important, why did the angel of God give such a grievous judgement to the wife of Lot? In Genesis 19:17 the Bible reads, "Escape for thy life; look not behind thee." It is a simple command: do not look behind you. However, when you read Genesis 19:26, you discover that Lot's wife looked back and became a pillar of salt. She received that grievous judgement just because she looked back.

You might say that the judgement was too harsh, but when you understand this law of the Spirit, it is not, for when she looked back, she did not only see with her physical eyes; when she looked, that sight came to her inner self, and gripped hold of her imagination. Lust for her former life began to take hold of her, and God carried out His just judgement upon her.

God has been using this language of the Holy Spirit to change many lives. Look carefully when you read Genesis 13:14–15, "And the Lord said unto Abraham, after that Lot was separated from him, 'Lift up now thine eyes, and look from the place where thou art, northward, southward, and eastward, and westward: For all the land which thou seest, to thee will I give it, and to thy seed forever.' "

God did not say, "Oh, Abraham, I'll give you Canaan. Just claim it." No, very specifically, God told him to stand from his place, look northward, southward, eastward, and westward, and that He would give that land to Abraham and his descendants.

I wish he could have had a helicopter, for then he could have gone up high and seen all the Middle East, and thus avoided the many past and present problems there. But since he had no binoculars and no helicopter, his vision was limited.

Seeing is possession. Abraham saw the land; he then went back to his tent, and to his bed, to dream of the lands which were going to become his. In his fourth dimension the Holy Spirit began to use that language. The Holy Spirit began to carry out dominion.

It is interesting that Abraham got his child Isaac when he was one hundred years old, and when Sarah was ninety. When Abraham was almost one hundred years old, and Sarah almost ninety, God came and told him that he was going to have a child. When God came to him and said, "You are going to have a son," Abraham laughed and laughed. This means that Abraham was totally unbelieving.

We also see that Sarah laughed behind the tent. God asked, "Sarah, why are you laughing?" She replied, "No, I didn't laugh." But God said, "No, you laughed."

Both Abraham and Sarah laughed. They were both unbelieving. But God had a way to make them believe, for God used the fourth dimension, the language of the Holy Spirit. One night God said to Abraham, "Come out." In the Middle East the humidity is very low, so in the night you can see the many stars sparkling. Abraham came out, and God said, "Abraham, count the number of the stars." So he started counting the stars.

Scientists say that with the human eye we can count 6,000 stars. So we can imagine Abraham kept on counting and counting, eventually forgetting the number. He finally said, "Father, I can't count them all." Then the Father said, "Your children are going to become as numerous as those stars."

I imagine that Abraham was struck with emotion. Soon tears began to well up in his eyes, and his vision became completely blurred. When he looked up at the stars, all he could see were the faces of his children, and suddenly he felt that he was hearing them call to him, "Father Abraham!" He was all shaken up, and when he returned to his tent he was shaking all over. He could not sleep when he closed his eyes, for he saw all the stars changing into the faces of his descendants, and once again shouting, "Father Abraham!"

Those pictures came to his mind again and again, and became his own dreams and pictures. Those pictures immediately became part of his fourth dimension, in the language of spiritual visions and dreams. These visions and dreams carried dominion over his one-hundred-year-old body, and it was soon transformed as if it were like a young body. From that time on he believed the Word of God, and he praised the Lord.

Who could change Abraham so much? The Holy Spirit, because God had applied the law of the fourth dimension, the language of the Holy Spirit. A vision and dream changed Abraham, not only his mind, but his physical body as well – not only he, but his wife, too, were wonderfully rejuvenated. Later on in the Bible you can read how King Abimelech tried to make Sarah his concubine: ninety-year-old Sarah, who had been rejuvenated through the law and language of the fourth dimension.

We are not common animals. When God created us He created in us the fourth dimension, the spiritual world. Then God said, "You carry out dominion over all the third dimension."

I cannot carry out my ministry of winning souls by simply knocking on doors, struggling and working myself to death. I use the way of faith, and the church is growing by leaps and bounds. And even though our church has more than 50,000 registered members, when I go to the office I do not have a great deal to do, for I follow a path of faith, and am not constantly striving in my flesh to bring to pass those things that the Holy Spirit can easily do.

I learned that even while I minister in foreign countries I can go into the fourth dimension of the Holy Spirit, and I tell Him what is needed in my church in Korea, and He carries out the work. I call my wife about every two days, and she is continually giving me information which has served sometimes as a blow to my ego. I used to think that the members of my church would be very anxious for my return from my trips abroad; they would all be waiting for me, and I was sure that Sunday service attendance would go down. She would say, "Don't brag about it. The church is doing all the better, even without having you."

Applying the Law of the Fourth Dimension

If God could use Abraham to possess the land through the miraculous fourth dimension, and if God could rejuvenate Abraham and Sarah through the Holy Spirit's language of visions and dreams, then you can also work in the fourth dimension.

There is a magnificent story about Jacob in Genesis 30:31–43. I had always disliked the portion of scripture in verses 37 through 39, where Jacob made an arrangement to ensure that solid colored cattle would give birth to spotted and speckled cattle.

I asked, "Lord, why do you permit this superstition in the Bible? This is the reason the Modernists are criticizing the Bible, and calling it a fairy story."

So whenever I came to this part of Scripture, I would skip it, fearing and worrying that there was a portion of the Bible I could not trust. One day while reading the Bible under the anointing of the Holy

Spirit, I again came to these verses and said, "I'm going to skip this part. This is all superstition."

But the Holy Spirit said, "Wait a minute. Nothing in the Bible is superstition. The matter is that you don't understand. You are blind, but I am applying the special law of creation here. You watch."

Then a tremendous unveiling of truth came to me, and this added a new dimension to my ministry. If you do not use the miraculous laws of faith you cannot hope to see a thousand new members added to your church each month; your personal struggle apart from the working of the fourth dimension cannot bring this goal about.

In this part of his life, Jacob, whose name meant "the swindler," had gone to his Uncle Laban. He stayed for about twenty years, working as hard as a common labourer for his uncle. But his uncle changed the salary so many times that Jacob was being deceived; Jacob was in turn also deceiving his uncle. They were deceiving each other, and when Jacob became about forty years old, he had nothing in the way of material gain, but did have a lot of wives and children, and a desire to return home.

God felt sorry for Jacob, and showed him a portion of the secret of the fourth dimension. After receiving this revelation from the Lord, Jacob went to his uncle. He said, "Uncle, I'll work for you on this condition: you take away all the spotted and speckled animals from me, and I'll tend only the animals with coats of solid colors. And if someway these solid colored animals give birth to spotted and speckled offspring, then those would become my salary."

Jacob's uncle almost jumped. He thought to himself, "Oh, now this guy is cheating himself. Those solid colored animals have a very slim chance of giving birth to many of the spotted and speckled offspring. Now I can use him without paying much salary."

So Jacob's uncle said to him, "Yes, yes. That's wonderful. I'll make that contract with you."

Then Laban took all the spotted and speckled animals and removed them three days distance away, and Jacob was left with only the animals of solid color. Jacob went out to the mountain, cut down poplar, hazel and chestnut trees, and with his penknife made them all spotted and speckled. He made a wall out of those now spotted and speckled tree rods, and put that wall right in front of the cattle's drinking trough, where the cattle would drink and come to conceive offspring.

There Jacob would stand, day in and day out, watching the animals in front of those spotted and speckled tree rods. The Bible says that soon afterward all those animals gave birth to spotted and speckled offspring.

God created a vision and dream in the mind of

Jacob. His subconscious before had been full of poverty, failure, and cheating; so his struggle was hard, and his rewards few. But God changed Jacob's imagination, his subconscious, by using this wall of spotted and speckled tree rods as material to help him visualize and dream.

Jacob looked at that wall so much that his mind became filled with the sight; he slept and dreamed dreams of the cattle giving birth to spotted and speckled offspring. In the next chapter we read that the cattle did give birth to spotted and speckled offspring. Man's imagination plays a great role in the fourth dimension. Animals can never have an imagination in the way we do, because imagination is the work of the spirit.

When in Jacob's heart and imagination he began to grasp this vision and dream of spotted and speckled cattle, he began to learn the language of the Holy Spirit. You can converse with another person only through a known language, and you can never converse with an unknown language.

When Jacob began to learn the language of the Holy Spirit, immediately he began to converse with the Holy Spirit, and the Holy Spirit began to work. The Holy Spirit punched the proper keys for the necessary genes, and Jacob's cattle began to give birth to spotted and speckled offspring. Jacob soon began to have a vast multitude of spotted and speckled animals, and he became one of the richest men in the Orient.

There are over 8,000 promises in the Bible, and each of those promises is like a spotted and speckled tree for you. You do not need to go to the mountain to cut down a hazel, or a chestnut, or a poplar tree. You can rather take the promises from the Bible, all spotted and speckled, waiting for you. These promises, however, are a bit different, for these promises are all spotted and speckled by the blood of Jesus Christ.

Long after Jacob, God put up another spotted and speckled tree; this time that tree was on Calvary. And this tree was not spotted and speckled by a pen-knife, but by the real blood of the Son of God. Anybody and everybody can come gaze upon this spotted and speckled tree, and receive a new image, a new dream, and a new vision, by the power of the Holy Spirit, and be changed.

Now let me share something from my personal experience with you. One Christmas Eve I was busy preparing a sermon. Later an urgent telephone call came in the early morning hours of Christmas day. A man calling from Seoul National Hospital asked, "Are you Pastor Cho?"

"Yes, I am."

"One of your members is dying. He was in a car accident. A taxi hit him, then rode around all through the morning with him in the back seat."

In Korea at that time, if someone was hit and killed by a taxi, the taxi-driver would only have to pay the sum of $2500, and then would be cleared of all financial obligation. However, if the victim were only injured, then the driver would have to pay for all of the medical and hospital bills. So if a driver hit someone and no one saw the accident, he would then drive that person around until he or she died; it would be cheaper for him.

This member had bought a beautiful hat, with some other articles, for his wife. He was so carried away with the joy of giving these presents, that he jay-walked across the street without watching the light, and was hit by a taxi. Since it was late evening and no one saw, this taxi-driver had carried that man in his car throughout the evening. The man did not die, and eventually a policeman caught the taxi, and carried the man to a hospital. The impact of the accident had badly impaired his intestines, and his stomach was full of dirt and blood; blood poisoning had already set in.

His doctor knew me and called, saying, "Dr. Cho, should we operate on him? Medically speaking, it's hopeless. He was without medical attention for such a long time that blood poisoning has set in. There will be no way for us to cure him."

But I said, "You go ahead and operate on him, and as soon as I finish the Christmas sermon, I'll run to the hospital."

After the Christmas service I rushed to the emergency room of Seoul National University Hospital, and there he was, totally unconscious. The doctor again said there would be no hope, "Reverend, don't expect anything. He is dying. We could do nothing. When we opened his stomach, there were three places where the intestines were completely cut off, and these areas were filled with his excrement and dirt. There is no hope."

I replied, "Well, I'll try to do my best."

When I went in he was in a deep coma. I knelt beside him and said, "Lord God, give me only five minutes, then I will try. Let him come out of the coma for five minutes, then I will try."

As I was praying I felt something moving. I opened my eyes, and the man opened his eyes.

"Oh, pastor, I'm dying," he cried.

I knew then that I had five minutes. I replied, "You can't say that. As long as you keep saying that you will die, then I can't help you. You must change your imagination and thinking. Change your vision and dream, for the only way to carry out dominion over this third dimension material world is through your imagination, your visions and dreams.

"So listen to me. Picture a young man. He says good-bye to his wife. He's full of beauty and health. He goes to his office, and completes his business successfully.

"All the people respect and admire him. Evening arrives and he buys nice gifts for his wife, who is waiting for him to come home and eat supper. When he arrives she rushes out to the gate and welcomes him with a big hug and kiss. They go into the house, share a delicious meal together, and a quiet evening at home.

"The man I am talking about is no stranger. That man is you! Think of that man! Draw that picture in your mind. Look at that man and say in your heart, that man is me!

"Don't draw a picture of death. Don't draw a picture of a dead corpse. Keep on dreaming about that man, and I'll do the praying. You just draw a mental picture, and leave the praying to me. Will you do that?"

"Yes, pastor, I'll change my dream. I'll change my thinking. I'll say that I'm that man. I'll try to make that vision and dream a reality...I see it!" he cried.

While we were talking this surgeon had come in with his nurses. They started giggling and laughing at me, and thought that I had lost my mind. But I was serious, for I knew the law of the Spirit's fourth dimension, and that man had begun to speak the language of the Holy

Spirit. Like a missionary on a foreign field who gains a deeper level of communication with the local people of that country by learning to speak their language directly, instead of using an interpreter, so that dying man had learned the deeper language of the Holy Spirit.

As I knelt down and grabbed hold of his bed, I prayed, "Dear Holy Spirit, now he speaks your language. He has a vision and a dream. Rush into his physical body, and carry out your dominion. I command this man to be whole and to be filled with healing power!"

Suddenly the group of unbelieving nurses said, "This room is too hot. The heat is too high."

But the weather was very cold. There was no heat; it was the power of the Holy Spirit giving off all the heat. The surgeon and those nurses began to feel fire. Their ears turned red, and the power of God became so strong that we even felt the bed trembling.

Amazingly, in one week that man rose up and walked out of the hospital. He is now in the chemical business, doing wonderfully. Whenever I see him on Sunday morning, sitting in the balcony, I say to myself, "Praise God! We spoke the Holy Spirit's language. We created. Hallelujah!"

Let me tell you about another incident. One day I was in my office, and a lady about 50 years old came in crying: "Pastor, my home is completely destroyed and broken."

"Stop crying," I responded, "and tell me about it."

"You know we have several sons, but only one daughter. She has become a hippie, and she sleeps with friends of my husband and with friends of my sons, going from this hotel to that hotel, and from this dance hall to that dance hall.

"She's become a shame to our family," she cried. "My husband cannot go to his office. My boys are dying of embarrassment, and now they are all going to leave home. I've tried everything. I've even cried to the Lord to strike her dead! Oh, Pastor Cho, what can I do?"

"Stop whining and crying," I told her. "I now can see very clearly why God would not answer your prayer. You were presenting the wrong kind of mental blueprint to Him. In your mind you were always submitting just the picture of a prostitute, weren't you?"

She retorted, "Yes, well, that's what she is. She is a prostitute!"

"But if you want to see her changed, then you must submit another mental blueprint," I told her. "You must clean the canvas of your imagination, and you must start drawing a new picture."

But she rejected the idea, saying, "I can't. She's dirty, ugly and wretched."

"Stop talking like that. Let's draw a new picture. Let's bring to mind another kind of spotted and speckled tree. You kneel down here, and I will kneel down before you. Let's go to the foot of Calvary. Let's lift up our hands. Let's look at Jesus Christ dying on a cross, bleeding and beaten up.

"Why is He hanging there? Because of your daughter. Let's put your daughter right behind Jesus Christ. Let's see your daughter through His spotted and speckled cross. Can't you see your daughter forgiven, cleansed, born again, and filled with the Holy Spirit—completely changed? Can you draw that picture through the blood of Jesus Christ?"

"Oh, pastor, yes," replied the mother. "Now I see differently. Through Jesus, through the cross, I can change my image about my daughter."

"Wonderful, wonderful!" I exclaimed. "I will draw a new picture of your daughter. Keep that clear-cut, vivid and graphic picture in your mind day in and day out. Then the Holy Spirit can use you, for His language is carried with a vision and a dream. We know we are drawing the right kind of picture since we are coming to the foot of the cross."

So we knelt down and prayed, "Oh Lord, now you see this picture. Dear Holy Spirit, flow into this new image, this new vision and dream. Change. Perform miracles."

Then I sent this mother out, and as she was leaving she was all smiles. There was no more crying, for her image of her daughter had changed.

One Sunday, a few months later, she suddenly walked into my office, bringing a beautiful young lady with her. "Who is this young lady?" I asked.

"This is my daughter!" she smiled.

"Did God answer you?"

She replied, "Oh yes, He did."

Then she told me the story. One night her daughter had been sleeping in a motel with a man. In the morning when she woke up she felt dirty and wretched. She felt a great unhappiness in her spirit, and had a deep desire to return home, but she was frightened and scared of her parents and brothers. Nevertheless, she decided to risk it, saying to herself, "I'll try one more time, and if they kick me out, then that will be my last attempt."

So she went to her parents' home and rang the bell. Her mother came out, and when she saw her daughter, her countenance lit up as if the sun was rising on her face. She greeted her daughter, "Welcome, my daughter," and rushed out to hug her.

The daughter was absolutely overwhelmed by the love of her mother, and she crumbled, crying. Her mother had prayed, and her image of her daughter was entirely changed. She had welcomed her daughter on the spot, and opened wide her arms of love.

Her mother brought her to the church for a period of two or three months. She listened to the sermons, confessed all sins, gave her heart to Jesus Christ, and received the baptism of the Holy Spirit. She became an absolutely new creation in Christ, and she eventually found a wonderful husband.

This daughter now has three children of her own, and is one of the foremost home cell unit leaders in my church. She is a burning evangelist; and all this happened because her mother changed her vision and dream, applying the law of the fourth dimension.

Throughout Scripture God always made use of this law of the fourth dimension. Look at Joseph. Before he was sold as a slave God had already imprinted in his heart pictures in the fourth dimension. Through several dreams God gave a clear-cut vision to the heart of Joseph. Even though Joseph was taken as a slave to Egypt, he was already carrying dominion over his faith. Joseph later became a prime minister.

Look at Moses. Before he built the tabernacle he was called to Mount Sinai. He stayed there for forty days and nights, and was given a mental picture of the tabernacle; exactly as he saw it in his vision and dream he went and built it.

God gave visions to Isaiah, to Jeremiah, to Ezekiel and to Daniel, all major servants of the Lord. God called them into the fourth dimension, and taught them the language of the Holy Spirit. They then made the prayer of faith.

This was true even of the Apostle Peter. His original name was Simon, meaning "a reed." When Peter came, led by Andrew, Jesus looked into his eyes and laughed. "Yes, you are the Simon. You are the reed. Your personality is so bendable, changeable. In one moment you are angry; in another you laugh. Sometimes you get drunk, and at other times you show how intelligent you can be.

"You really are like a reed, but I am going to call you a rock. Simon, a reed, is dead to the world, and Peter, the rock, is alive."

Peter was a fisherman and knew the strong and stable qualities of a rock. In his imagination he immediately began to see himself portrayed as a rock. He would watch as the wind-tossed waves of the Sea of Galilee would hit a rock, engulfing it with white foam; and the rock looked conquered. But in the next moment he would see all the water breaking against the rock, and sliding off, and the rock still stood. Peter again and again said, "Am I like the rock? Am I? Yes, I am like a rock."

Peter became a strong rock of the Early Church. But before he was changed into this rock, Christ saw a vision of Peter as a rock in His heart, and then he became that rock.

God changed the name of Jacob to Israel, meaning "the prince of God." He was a cheater and swindler, but he was named a prince. It was after then that he changed.

Non-Christians from all over the world are involved in transcendental meditation and Buddhistic meditation. In meditation one is asked to have a clear-cut goal and vision. In Sokagakkai they draw a picture of prosperity, repeating phrases over and over, trying to develop the human spiritual fourth dimension; and these people are creating something. While Christianity has been in Japan for more than 100 years, with only 0.5 percent of the population claiming to be Christians, Sokagakkai has millions of followers. Sokagakkai has applied the law of the fourth dimension and has performed miracles; but in Christianity there is only talk about theology and faith.

People are created in the image of God. God is a God of miracles, His children, therefore, born with the desire to see miracles performed. Without seeing miracles people cannot be satisfied that God is powerful.

Your Responsibility

It is you who are responsible to supply miracles for these people. The Bible is not of the third dimension, but of the fourth, for in it we can read of God, and the life He has for us, and can learn the language of the Holy Spirit. By reading Scripture you can enlarge your visions and your dreams. Make your dreams and your visions, and create. Let the Holy Spirit come and quicken the scriptures you read, and implant visions in the young and dreams in the old.

If you lack the mobility and opportunity of a missionary, then at least you can sit in your chair and dream. That is powerful. Let the Holy Spirit come and teach you the language of the Holy Spirit, the language of visions and dreams. Then keep those visions, keep those dreams, and let the Holy Spirit flow through that language, and create.

God wants to give you the desires of your heart. God is ready to fulfill those desires, because the Bible says, "Delight thyself in the Lord, and He shall give thee the desires of thine heart." Also in Proverbs 10:24, "The desire of the righteous shall be granted." First make a clear-cut goal, then draw a mental picture, vivid and graphic, and become enthusiastic, praying throughout the process. Do not be deceived by the talk of mind expansion, yoga, transcendental meditation, or Sokagakkai. They are only developing the human fourth dimension, and in these cases are not in the good, but rather the evil, fourth dimension.

Let us rise up and do more than an Egyptian magician. There are plenty of magicians in the Egypts of this world, but let us use all our visions and our dreams for our Holy God. Let us become Moses, and go out and perform the most wonderful of miracles.

Miracles are a usual and expected occurrence in our church, so by experience I can say that man is not just another animal. You are not a common creature, for you have the fourth dimension in your heart, and it is the fourth dimension that has dominion over the three material dimensions—the cubical world, the world of the plane, and the world of the line.

Through dominion in the fourth dimension—the realm of faith—you can give order to your circumstances and situations, give beauty to the ugly and chaotic, and healing to the hurt and suffering.

3

THE CREATIVE POWER OF THE SPOKEN WORD

There are certain steps we must follow for faith to be properly incubated, and a central truth we must learn about the realm that faith operates in; there is also a basic principle about the spoken word that we need to understand. So I want to speak to you about the creative power of the spoken word, and the reasons why the usage of it is of such importance.

One morning I was eating breakfast with one of Korea's leading neuro-surgeons, who was telling me about various medical findings on the operation of the brain. He asked, "Dr. Cho, did you know that the speech center in the brain rules over all the nerves? You ministers really have power, because according to our recent findings in neurology, the speech center in the brain has total dominion over all the other nerves."

Then I laughed, saying, "I've known that for a long time."

"How did you know that?" he asked. "In the world of neurology these are new findings."

I replied that I had learned it from Dr. James.

"Who is this Dr. James?" he asked.

"He was one of the famous doctors in biblical times,

nearly two thousand years ago," I replied. "And in his book, chapter three, the first few verses, Dr. James clearly defines the activity and importance of the tongue and the speech center."

The neuro-surgeon was completely amazed. "Does the Bible really teach about this?"

"Yes," I answered. "The tongue is the least member of our body, but can bridle the whole body."

Then this neuro-surgeon began to expound their findings. He said that the speech nerve center had such power over all of the body that simply speaking can give one control over his body, to manipulate it in the way he wishes. He said, "If someone keeps on saying, 'I'm going to become weak,' then right away, all the nerves receive that message, and they say, 'Oh, let's prepare to become weak, for we've received instructions from our central communication that we should become weak.' They then in natural sequence adjust their physical attitudes to weakness.

"If someone says, 'Well, I have no ability. I can't do this job,' then right away all the nerves begin to declare the same thing. 'Yes,' they respond, 'we received instruction from the central nervous system saying that we have no abilities, to give up striving to develop any capacity for capability. We must prepare ourselves to be part of an incapable person.'

"If someone keeps saying, 'I'm very old. I'm so very old, and am tired and can't do anything,' then right away, the speech central control responds, giving out orders to that effect. The nerves respond, 'Yes, we are old. We are ready for the grave. Let's be ready to disintegrate.' If someone keeps saying that he is old, then that person is soon going to die."

That neuro-surgeon continued saying, "That man should never retire. Once a man retires, he keeps repeating to himself, 'I am retired,' and all the nerves start responding and become less active, and ready for a quick death."

For a Successful Personal Life

That conversation carried much meaning for me, and made an impact on my life, for I could see that one important usage of the spoken word is the creation of a successful personal life.

People easily adapt to speaking in a negative way. "Boy, am I poor. I've even no money to give the Lord." When an opportunity does come for a job with a good salary, the nervous system responds, "I am not able to be rich because I haven't received that reverse instruction from my nerve center yet. I am supposed to be poor, so I can't accept this job. I can't afford to have the money." Like attracts like, and since you act as if you were a poor person, you attract poverty; this attraction, if it remains consistent, will allow you to permanently dwell in poverty.

Exactly as the Bible said nearly 2,000 years ago, it is so today. Medical science has just recently discovered this principle. This one neuro-surgeon said that people should keep saying to themselves, "I am young. I am able. I can do the work of a young person no matter what my chronological age is." The nerves of that person will then come alive and thus receive power and strength from the nerve center.

The Bible says clearly that whosoever controls the tongue, controls the whole body. What you speak, you are going to get. If you keep on saying that you are poor, then all of your system conditions itself to attract poverty, and you will feel at home in poverty; you would rather be poor. But if you keep on saying that you are able, that you can achieve success, then all of your body would be bridled to success. You would be ready to meet any challenge, ready to conquer it. This is the reason you should never speak in a negative way.

In Korea we have a habit of making frequent use of words having to do with dying. Common expressions are: "Oh, it's so warm I could die;" "Oh, I've eaten so much I could suffocate to death;" "Oh, I'm so happy I could die;" and "Oh, I'm scared to death." Koreans repeatedly use these negative words. That is the reason that throughout Korea's five thousand year history we have been constantly dying, constantly at war. My generation has never seen total peace in our country. I was born during World War II, grew up during the Korean War, and now still live in a country on the brink of war.

Before you can be changed, you must change your language. If you do not change your language, you cannot change yourself. If you want to see your children changed, you must first teach them to use the proper language. If you want to see rebellious and irresponsible youth changed into responsible adults, you must teach them this new language.

Where can we learn this new language? From the best language book of all, the Bible. Read the Bible from Genesis to Revelation. Acquire the Bible's language, speak the word of faith, and feed your nervous system with a vocabulary of constructive, progressive, productive and victorious words. Speak those words; keep repeating them, so that they will have control of your whole body. Then you will become victorious, for you will be completely conditioned to meet your environment and circumstances, and achieve success. This is the first important reason to use the spoken word: to create the power to have a successful personal life.

For God's Purposes

There is a second reason we need to use the creative power of the spoken word: not only can it help us to be successful in our own lives, but the Holy Spirit also needs us to use it to bring about God's purposes.

When I first entered the ministry I could feel myself in a struggle, even while I delivered my sermons, and sensed hindrances in my spirit. Then the Spirit of the Lord would come down into my spirit, and it would be as if I were watching television. On my mind's screen I could see growths disappear, tuberculosis healed, cripples leaning heavily on crutches suddenly throw them aside and walk.

Korea is such a distance from America, that I heard very little about this type of deliverance and healing ministry. Even the few missionaries around me then were ignorant of this type of ministry, and talking to them resulted in my being even more confused.

I came to the conclusion that this was a hindrance created by satan. Each time it would happen I would say, "You spirit of hindrance, get out of me. I command you to leave me. Get out of me."

But the more I commanded, the more clearly I

could envision people being healed. I became so desperate I could hardly preach. The visions constantly appeared, so I made it a matter of fasting and prayer, waiting upon the Lord.

Then in my heart I heard the Lord say, "Son, that is not a hindrance of satan. That is the visual desire of the Holy Spirit. It is the Word of wisdom and of knowledge. God wants to heal these people, but God can't heal them before you speak."

"No," I replied, "I don't believe that. God can do anything without my ever saying a word."

Later I saw in the Bible, the first chapter of Genesis, "The earth was without form and void," and the Holy Spirit brooded over the earth, incubating it; but nothing happened. God then revealed an important truth to me. He said, "There was the presence of the Holy Spirit, the mighty anointing of the Holy Ghost incubating and brooding over the waters. Did anything happen at that point?"

"No," I replied. "Nothing happened."

Then God spoke, "You can feel the presence of the Holy Spirit in your church—the pulsating, permeating presence of the Holy Spirit—but nothing will happen— no soul will be saved, no broken home rejoined, until you speak the word. Don't just beg and beg for what you need. Give the word. Let me have the material with which I can build miraculous happenings. As I did when creating the world, speak forth. Say 'let there be light,' or say, 'let there be firmament.' "

The realization of that truth was a turning point in my life. I then apologized to God: "Lord, I'm sorry. I'll speak forth."

But still I was afraid, for no one had taught me anything along these lines. I was also scared that nothing would happen when I spoke forth; then what would people say about me? So I said to God, "Since I'm afraid, I'm not going to speak out about the cripples I see healed, or the disappearing cancer tumors. Father, I'll start with headaches."

After this when I preached, visions of healings would spring up from my spirit; but when in my mind's eye I could see cripples healed, or tumors disappearing, I ignored them. I would speak forth, "Someone here is being healed of a headache." And instantly that person would be healed. I was amazed that just by my speaking these things they would come into being.

Little by little I gained more courage. I began to speak of sinuses that had been healed, then of the healing of the deaf, and finally spoke of all the healings I saw pictured in my mind. Now in my church on Sunday mornings hundreds of people receive healing through that channel. Because time is so limited, because of the multiple services, I must act quickly. So while I am standing, the Lord shows me the healings that are taking place, and I call them out. I simply close my eyes and speak forth. In recognition of the fact that they have been healed, people stand up. They stand when the particular disease or illness of which they have been healed is called out. During this portion of a service many people, all over the auditorium, rise to claim their healing.

Thus I learned one secret: before you give the word, the Holy Spirit does not have the proper material with which to create. If the Holy Spirit imparts faith into your heart to remove a mountain, do not pray and beg for the mountain to be moved; rather speak, "Be removed to yonder sea!" and it shall come to pass. If you learn this, and make it a habit to speak under the Holy Spirit's anointing, and in the faith God gives you, then you are going to see many miracles in your life.

Ministering to 50,000 regular attending members is not an easy task. We have set up a 24 hour telephone service in our church, and assistants stay round-the-clock to receive calls and instructions. I try to keep my home phone number unregistered, but that unregistered number soon becomes known, and I receive telephone calls from the early part of the evening till late the next morning.

Many nights I will be lying cozily in bed. Then at ten o'clock a telephone call will come: "Pastor, my grandson has a high fever, please pray for him." So I pray.

Eleven o'clock another telephone call comes: "My husband still isn't home from his business. Please pray," and I pray.

Then at twelve o'clock midnight, the phone rings and a crying wife says, "My husband came home and beat me up. Oh, this is terrible. I don't want to live." Then I will counsel with her.

One o'clock I receive a call from a drunken man saying, "My wife attends your church: why do you teach her to behave in such a way?" Then I will give him a full explanation.

In mid-morning a telephone call comes from the hospital, "Pastor, such and such a person is dying now. Would you come quickly? His last desire before dying is to see you." So I make plans to rush to the hospital.

The telephone keeps ringing so much that at times I have just unplugged the cord. I exclaim, "I'm not going to live this way!" Then I go to bed.

But then the Holy Spirit speaks to my heart. "Are you being a good shepherd? A good shepherd never leaves his sheep stranded." So I rise up and push the cord back in. There is one advantage I have when traveling out of my country: I can finally get a good night's sleep.

On one particular evening during a very cold winter night, when I was feeling so good and cozy in my bed, just about to fall asleep, a telephone call came. This man I had met called saying, "Pastor, do you know me?"

"Of course I know you. I married you and your wife."

"I have tried for two years, with my entire might, but our marriage is not working out," he said. "Tonight we had a big argument and decided to separate. We've already divided our assets, but there's just one thing – a blessing from you. We were married with your blessing and we want to be divorced with your blessing."

What a position for a minister to be in, to bless them in joining, and then bless them in dis-joining! I replied, "Can you wait till tomorrow? It's too cold, and I'm settled in bed. Must I come now?"

"Pastor," he returned, "tomorrow will be too late. We're leaving each other today. We don't want you to preach to us. It's too late for that, we're beyond reach now; just come and simply give us your blessing so that we can be divorced."

I crawled out of my bed and went into the living

room. In my heart I was angry against satan. I thought, "This is not the work of the Holy Spirit. This is the work of the devil."

As I began to pray I immediately went into the fourth dimension. Since visions and dreams are the language of the Holy Spirit, through the fourth dimension I can incubate the third dimension, and correct it. I knelt down, closed my eyes, and through the cross of Jesus Christ, by the help of the Holy Spirit, I began to see this family rejoined together again. I envisioned a clear picture, and prayed, "Oh, God, make it like that."

While praying I was touched by faith, and in the name of Jesus Christ changed this situation in the fourth dimension. The fourth dimension with its positive power was mine, so I went to this couple's apartment.

They were living in a fantastically luxurious apartment. There was every convenience in that apartment, but when I walked in, I felt an icy chill, the hatred that existed between that man and his wife. You can have all the material goods of this world, but if there is hatred in your family, those material things will be no blessing at all.

As I came in I found the man sitting in the living room and the wife in the bedroom. As soon as I walked into the living room the man began to speak derogatorily about his wife. His wife then rushed into the room saying, "Don't listen to him! Listen to me!" Then she also began to speak out against her husband.

I would listen to the husband, and everything that he said seemed to be right. Then I would listen to the wife, and everything that she said seemed to be right; each was right in his own opinion. Both were right, and I was sandwiched between.

Both said they were completely finished in their marriage. "Don't pray for us," they kept repeating. "Just pray for our divorce."

But I had already overruled this third dimension decision by using the fourth dimension in my heart. Being confident, I took the hand of the husband and the hand of the wife, and I said, "In the name of Jesus Christ, I command satan to loose his hold of hatred on this couple. And in this moment, in the mighty name of Jesus Christ I command that these two be melted together. Let them be tender and rejoined."

Suddenly I felt a warm drop fall on my hand, and when I looked at the man he was crying, and his tears were falling down.

I thought to myself, "Oh, praise God! It worked!"

When I looked at the eyes of the wife I could see that her eyes were watering also. So I drew their hands together and said, "What the Lord has joined, let no man or circumstances divide."

I stood up and said, "I'm going."

Both of them followed me out to the gate, and as I left said, "Good-bye, Pastor."

"Praise God," I replied, "it works!"

The next Sunday both of them sat in the choir and sang beautifully. After the service I shook their hands and asked the wife, "What happened?"

"Well, we don't know," she answered. "But when you said those words and gave such strong commands, we felt something break down in our hearts. It was as if a wall had been destroyed, and we were shaken.

"Suddenly we began to be conscious that perhaps we should try once again, both at the same time. After you left, we spent the entire night unpacking all of our things. Now when we think of it, we can't understand why we argued so much, and why we were going to separate. Now we love each other even more than before."

The Holy Spirit needs both your word and mine. If I had pleaded with them or if I had silently prayed for them, I would have missed the target. I gave the word, and the word went out and created. The Holy Spirit needs your definite word, the spoken word of faith.

Jesus used the spoken word to change and create. The disciples of Christ Jesus used the spoken word to change and create. Unfortunately the Church of Jesus Christ seems to have become a perennial beggar: begging and begging, afraid to speak forth the words of command. We need to learn the lost art of speaking forth the word of command.

For the Release of the Presence of Christ

There is a third reason to use the power of the spoken word: through it you create and release the presence of Jesus Christ. When you open the Bible and read Romans 10:10 you find that "with the heart man believeth unto righteousness; and with the mouth confession is made unto salvation." It is through confession of faith that man can grasp the salvation that comes only by Jesus Christ.

Now nowhere in this passage is it necessary that someone send up to heaven and bring Jesus Christ down to earth to give salvation. What is said is that the words which can result in salvation are near, for they are the words in your heart and in your mouth.

Where is Jesus Christ in this process? What is His address? Not high up in the sky, or below the ground. Jesus is in His Word.

Where are the words that can result in your salvation? Those words are on your mouth and in your heart. Jesus is bound to what you speak forth. As well as you can release Jesus' power through your spoken word, you can also create the presence of Christ. If you do not speak the word of faith clearly, Christ can never be released. The Bible says that "whatsoever you bind on earth shall be bound in heaven, and whatsoever you release on earth shall be released in heaven." You have the responsibility of carrying the presence of Jesus Christ.

Whenever I have a session with my 100 assistant pastors of our church, I give them a strict command: "It's your responsibility to create the presence of Jesus Christ wherever you go. To release Jesus and to meet specific needs is what you must do." Let me give you some examples.

In our vicinity there are several churches belonging to various denominations. In one particular Presbyterian church the minister speaks only about the born again experience. He speaks strongly only about the salvation experience, so he is just releasing and creating the presence of the Jesus who can give this born again experience to people. People come to his church and they receive salvation, but no more than that.

The Holiness Church next door speaks day in and day out about sanctification. "Be sanctified, be sanctified," they repeatedly exhort. Many people come and receive the touch of sanctification. The minister there is only creating the presence of the sanctifying Christ.

But in my church I preach about the saving Jesus,

the sanctifying Christ, the baptising Saviour, the blessing Son of God, and the healing Jesus; and we have all of these aspects manifested in my church. I try to create the whole presence, the rounded out presence, of Jesus Christ.

Your Role

You create the presence of Jesus with your mouth. If you speak about salvation, the saving Jesus appears. If you speak about divine healing, then you will have the healing Christ in your congregation. If you speak the miracle performing Jesus, then the presence of the miracle performing Jesus is released. He is bound by your lips and by your words. He is depending on you, and if you do not speak clearly because of your fear of satan, how will Jesus Christ manifest His power to this generation? So speak boldly.

Many people have great problems in their homes because they do not have family altars. If the father maintains a family altar and speaks clearly about the presence of Jesus Christ in the home and in the family, he can create the presence of Jesus Christ, and Jesus can take care of all that family's problems. But since many neglect the family altar, they neglect speaking the clear presence of Jesus Christ, and their children are left without the full blessings of God.

You do not need to wait until you receive any special spiritual gift. I have always said that spiritual gifts reside in the Holy Spirit. You, yourself, can never own a spiritual gift.

Suppose I had the gift of healing. Then indiscriminately I would heal everyone who sought me for healing. If I had the gift I would give to everyone; I would not be truly discerning. The Holy Spirit sees a need, and then allows the operation of a gift to flow through someone to meet that need.

It is important to remember that all the gifts reside in the Holy Spirit, for it is the Holy Spirit who dwells in your church, and dwells in you. Through Him you can have every type of ministry—the ministry of teaching, the ministry of evangelism, the ministry of missions, the ministry of pastoring, and the ministry of divine healing. Through you as His channel the Holy Spirit manifests Himself. So do not worry about your acquisition of any of the gifts.

Be bold. Receive the gift of boldness, then speak the word. Speak the word clearly, and create a specific presence of Jesus Christ. Release that specific presence of Jesus Christ to your congregation, and you are going to get specific results. A father can create the presence of Jesus Christ through his spoken word, and Jesus can take care of all his family's problems. So, in the same way, I come to my church to speak a message, and plant specific seeds to harvest specific results.

I see one great fault in American services. American pastors deliver fantastic messages to their congregations; but right afterward the people are dismissed and leave. They are not given time to bear the fruit those messages have brought to life. They receive all the spoken words of the message, but have no time to pray through, to get that word so implanted that it becomes a part of them.

In America services are dismissed too soon. Give the congregation time; shorten the preliminaries and entertainment. Give the Word, and let the people have more time to pray together. Let those spoken words be digested. If this were done you would see more results in these pastors' ministries.

Ultimately your word molds your life, for your speech center controls all the nerves. That is why speaking in another tongue is the initial sign of the baptism of the Holy Spirit. When the Holy Spirit takes over the speech center, He takes over all the nerves all over the body, and controls the entire body. So when we speak in other tongues we are filled with the Holy Spirit.

Speak the word to control and to bridle your whole body and your whole life. Give the word to the Holy

Spirit so that He can create something of it. Then create and release the presence of Jesus Christ through your spoken word.

Preach the word. The spoken word has power, and when you release that word, it is that word, and not you, who performs miracles.

God does not use you because you are completely sanctified, for as long as a Christian lives he will be struggling with the flesh. God uses you because you have faith. So brothers and sisters, let us make use of the spoken word—for success in our personal lives, for material with which the Holy Spirit can create, and for the purposes of creating and releasing the presence of Jesus Christ.

Remember that Christ is depending upon you and your spoken word to release His presence. What are you going to do with this Jesus who is riding on your tongue? Are you going to release Him for the blessing of others? Or are you going to lock Him up with a still tongue and a closed mouth? May God bless you as you make your decision.

4

RHEMA

The spoken word has powerful creativity, and its proper usage is vital to a victorious Christian life. This spoken word, however, must have a correct basis to be truly effective. The principle for discovering the correct basis for the spoken word is one of the most important portions of God's truth. It is concerning this topic that I want to share with you now.

Faith in God's Word: Problems and Productivity

One day a lady on a stretcher was carried into my office. She was paralysed from her neck down, and could not even move her fingers. As she was being carried into my office on a stretcher, I began to feel a strange sensation. It felt as if my heart was being troubled. Just as there was expectancy by the pool of Bethesda, I knew that something was going to happen.

I went beside her stretcher, and when I looked into her eyes I realized that she already had the faith to be healed: not a dead faith, but a living faith. I touched her forehead with my hand and said, "Sister, in the name of Jesus Christ, be healed."

Instantly the power of God came, and she was healed. She stood up from her stretcher, thrilled, frightened and amazed.

She later came to my house bringing gifts, and after entering my study she asked, "Could I please close the door?"

"Yes," I replied. "Close the door." Then she knelt down before me, still amazed that she had been healed, and said, "Sir, please reveal yourself to me. Are you the second incarnate Jesus?"

I laughed, "Dear sister, you know that I eat three meals a day, go to the bathroom, and sleep every night. I am as human as you are, and the only way I have salvation is through Jesus Christ."

This woman had received such a miraculous healing that word of it instantly spread. Soon afterward one rich woman came to the church, also being carried in by a stretcher. She had been a Christian for a long time, and a deaconess in the church. She had memorized scripture after scripture regarding divine healing: "I am the Lord that healeth thee" (Exodus 15:26); "With His stripes we are healed" (Isaiah 53:5); "He Himself took our infirmities, and bore our sicknesses" (Matthew 8:17); "And these signs shall follow them that believe ...they shall lay hands on the sick, and they shall recover" (Mark 16:17–18).

So I prayed for her with all my might, but nothing happened. Then I shouted, repeating the same prayers for healing. I used the Word of God, and I even jumped, but nothing happened. I asked her to stand up by faith. Many times she would stand, but the moment I took my hand away, she would fall down like a piece of dead wood. Then I would say, "Have more faith and stand up." Again she would stand up, and again she would fall down. She would then claim to me that she had all the faith in the world, but her faith never would work.

I became quite depressed, and eventually she began to cry. She claimed, "Pastor, you are prejudiced. You loved that other woman so much that you healed her. But you don't really love me. So I am still sick. You are prejudiced."

"Sister," I replied, "I have done everything. You saw me. I have prayed, I have cried, I have jumped, I have shouted. I did everything that a Pentecostal preacher can do, but nothing happened, and I can't understand it."

In my church this bothersome problem of one being healed while another remains ill has not limited itself to this one situation. World famous evangelists have come to my church and enthusiastically preached, "Everyone of you is going to be healed! Everyone of you!" They poured out words of faith, and many people would receive healing.

But then they would leave, receiving all the glory, and I would be left to contend with those not healed. These people would come to me, discouraged and cast down, and say, "We are not healed. God has given up on us; we are completely forgotten. Why should we continue to struggle to come to Jesus Christ and believe?"

I then travailed and cried, "Why Father? Why should it be like this? God, please give me the answer, a very clear-cut answer." And He did. So now I would like to share this answer with you, and some realizations that led me to this understanding.

People think that they can believe on the Word of God. They can. But they fail to differentiate between the Word of God which gives general knowledge about God, and the Word of God which God uses to impart faith about specific circumstances into a man's heart. It is this latter type of faith which brings miracles.

In the Greek language there are two different words for 'word,' *logos* and *rhema*. The world was created by the Word, *logos,* of God. *Logos* is the general Word of God, stretching from Genesis to Revelation, for all these books directly or indirectly tell about the Word, Jesus Christ. By reading the *logos* from Genesis to Revelation you can receive all the knowledge you need about God and His promises; but just by reading you do not receive faith. You have received knowledge and understanding about God, but you do not receive faith.

Romans 10:17 shows us that the material used to build faith is more than just reading God's Word: "Faith comes by hearing, and hearing by the Word of God." In this scripture 'word' is not *logos*, but *rhema*. Faith specifically comes by hearing the *rhema*.

In his Greek lexicon Dr. Ironside has defined *logos* as "the said word of God," and *rhema* as "the saying word of God." Many scholars define this action of *rhema* as being the Holy Spirit using a few verses of Scripture and quickening it personally to one individual person. Here is my definition of *rhema*: *rhema* is a specific word to a specific person in a specific situation.

Once in Korea a lady by the name of Yun Hae Kyung had a tremendous youth meeting on Samgak Mountain. She had a great ministry. When she stood up and people came forward, they would fall down, slain under the power of the Holy Spirit. Many young people would flock to her meetings, and when she held a youth campaign on Samgak Mountain, thousands of young people came to join in.

During the week of the youth campaign it rained heavily, and all the rivers overflowed. A group of young people wanted to go to the town on the opposite side of the river, where the meetings were being held. But when they came to the bank of the river, it was flooded. There was not a bridge or a boat to be seen, and most of them became discouraged.

But three girls got together and said, "Why can't we just wade through the water? Peter walked on the water, and Peter's God is our God, Peter's Jesus is our Jesus, and Peter's faith is our faith. Peter believed, and we should do all the more. We are going to go over this river!"

The river was completely flooded, but these three girls knelt down and held hands together, quoting the scriptures containing the story of Peter walking on the water, and they claimed they could believe in the same way. Then, in the sight of the rest of their group, they shouted and began to wade through the water.

Immediately they were swept away by an angry flood, and after three days their dead bodies were found in the open sea.

This incident caused repercussions throughout Korea. Non-Christian newspapers carried the story, making headlines of it: "Their God Could Not Save Them"; "Why Did God Not Answer Their Prayer of Faith?" So unbelievers had a real heyday as a result of this occurrence, and the Christian church experienced a slump, feeling depressed and discouraged, having no adequate answer.

This became a topic of discussion all over Korea, and many previously good Christians lost their faith. They would say, "These girls believed exactly as our ministers have taught; they exercised their faith. From the platform our pastors constantly urge the people to boldly exercise their faith in the Word of God. These girls did just that, so why didn't God answer? Jehovah God must not be a living God. This must just be a formalistic religion we have been involved in."

What kind of answer would you give to these people? Those girls had believed. They had exercised faith based on the Word of God.

But God had no reason to support their faith. Peter never walked on the water because of *logos*, which gives general knowledge about God. Peter required that Christ give a specific word to him: Peter asked, "Lord, if you are Jesus, command me to come."

Jesus replied, "Come."

The word Christ gave to Peter was not *logos*, but *rhema*. He gave a specific word, "Come," to a specific person, Peter, in a specific situation, a storm.

Rhema brings faith. Faith comes by hearing, and hearing by *rhema*. Peter never walked on the water by knowledge of God alone. Peter had *rhema*.

But these girls had only *logos*, a general knowledge of God, and in this case, the working of God through

Peter. They exercised their human faith on *logos*: that was their mistake. God, therefore, had no responsibility to support their faith, and the difference between the way these girls exercised faith and the way Peter exercised faith is as the difference between night and day.

Two years ago two Bible school graduates failed completely in their first venture into the ministry. These two fellows had been disciples of mine. They listened to my lectures, they came to my church and learned in concept the principles of faith.

They began their first venture into the ministry with what seemed to be a great deal of faith, clinging to such scriptures as: "Open your mouth wide and I will fill it" (Psalm 81:10); "If ye ask anything in my name, I will do it" (John 14:14).

They went to a bank and made a large loan. Then they went to a rich man and made another large loan. With this money they bought land and built a beautiful sanctuary—without even having a congregation. They began preaching, expecting the people to flock in by the hundreds, and their debts to be paid; but nothing like that happened.

One of these young ministers had borrowed approximately $30,000, the other about $50,000. Soon their creditors came to collect their payments, and these young men were cornered in a terrible situation, arriving at a point where they were near to losing their faith in God.

Then they both came to me. They cried, "Pastor Cho, why is your God and our God different? You started with $2,500, and now you have completed a five million dollar project. We went out and built things which cost only a total of $80,000. Why wouldn't God answer us? We believed in the same God, and we exercised the same faith. So why hasn't He answered?"

Then they started quoting scriptures containing promises from the Old Testament and New Testament, adding, "We did exactly as you taught and we failed."

Then I replied, "I am glad that you have failed after hearing my word. Surely you are *my* disciples, but you have not been the disciples of Jesus Christ. You misunderstood my teachings. I started my church because of *rhema,* not just *logos.* God clearly spoke to my heart, saying, "Rise up, go out and build a church which will seat 10,000 people. God imparted His faith to my heart, and I went out and a miracle occurred. But you went out just with *logos,* a general knowledge about God and His faith. God therefore has no responsibility to support you, even though your ministry was for the Lord Jesus Christ."

Brothers and sisters, through *logos* you can know

God. You can gain understanding and knowledge about Him. But *logos* does not always become *rhema*.

Suppose a sick man were to have gone to the pool of Bethesda and said to those around it, "You foolish fellows, why are you waiting here? This is always the same pool in the same location with the same water. Why should you wait here day after day? I'm just going to jump in and wash myself."

Then he might have dived in and washed himself. But if he were to come out of the water, he would not have been healed. It was only after the angel of the Lord came and troubled the water that the people could jump in, wash, and be healed. Yet it was still the same pool of Bethesda, at the same location, with the same water. Only when the water was troubled by God's angel could a miracle occur.

Rhema is produced out of *logos*. *Logos* is like the pool of Bethesda. You may listen to the Word of God and you may study the Bible, but only when the Holy Spirit comes and quickens a scripture or scriptures to your heart, burning them in your soul and letting you know that they apply directly to your specific situation, does *logos* become *rhema*.

Logos is given to everybody. *Logos* is common to Koreans, Europeans, Africans and Americans. It is given to all so that they may gain knowledge about

God; but *rhema* is not given to everyone. *Rhema* is given to that specific person who is waiting upon the Lord until the Holy Spirit quickens *logos* into *rhema*. If you never have time to wait upon the Lord, then the Lord can never come and quicken the needed scripture to your heart.

This is a busy age. People come to church and are entertained. They hear a short sermon and are dismissed, without having any time of waiting upon the Lord. They get the *logos*, but since they do not receive *rhema*, they miss out on seeing the miraculous workings of God, and begin to doubt His power.

People must come to the main sanctuary, listen attentively to the preacher, and wait upon the Lord. But they do not come and listen prayerfully to the preacher, waiting upon the Lord to receive *rhema*; therefore, they cannot receive the faith they need for the solutions to their problems. Their knowledge of the Bible increases as their problems increase, and though they come to church, nothing happens. So they begin to fall away and lose faith.

Another problem with many churches in this active age is that ministers are busy with too many matters. They spend hours and hours as a janitor, financier, constructor, and contractor, going in a hundred different directions.

By Saturday they are so tired that they fumble around trying to find some *logos* to preach on. They are so tired that they have no time to wait upon the Lord, no time to change the green grass into white milk. Their congregations are simply fed grass, and not even given the milk of the Word. This is a grave mistake.

Lay persons are not the pastor's enemies, but his friends. As did the apostles, so should the minister concentrate on prayer and the ministering of the Word of God, delegating any other type of work to his deacons, deaconesses and other lay leaders.

I follow this pattern in my church, and I dare not go up to the platform without first waiting upon the Lord and receiving the *rhema* God would have me give for that message. If I do not receive *rhema*, I will not go to the platform.

So I go up to Prayer Mountain on Saturday, crawl into a grotto, close the door, and wait there until the Holy Spirit comes and gives me the needed *rhema*. Sometimes I stay the whole night through, during that time praying, "Lord, tomorrow the people are coming with all kinds of problems – sickness, disease, family problems, problems in business—every type of problem that can be imagined.

"They are coming not only to hear general knowledge about You, but they are also coming to receive real sol-

utions to their problems. If we don't give them a living
faith, *rhema,* then they are going to go back home without receiving their solutions. I need to have a specific
message for a specific people at a specific time."

Then I wait until God gives me that message. When
coming to the platform, I march in like a general,
knowing that the message I preach is under the anointing of the Holy Spirit.

After I preach, people in the congregation come to
me and say, "Pastor, you preached exactly the word
I needed. I've got faith that my problem will be solved."
This is because I helped supply to them the *rhema.*

Brothers and sisters, we are not building a holy
country club in the church; we deal rather with matters
of life and death. If the pastor does not supply *rhema* to
his people, then you have just a religious social club.
In the social world already one can see organizations
such as Kiwanis Clubs and Rotary Clubs, and their
members pay a type of tithes, too.

The churches we build should be places where
people get their solutions from the Lord, receive
miracles for their lives, and can gain not just a knowledge about God, but get to know Him in a vital way.
In order to do this, the pastor must first receive *rhema.*

Christians should be given time to wait upon the
Lord, so that the Holy Spirit can have a full opportunity

to deal with their lives and inspire them through the Scripture. The Holy Spirit can take Scripture, the "said word" of God, and apply it to a person's heart, making it the "saying word" of God. The *logos* then becomes the *rhema*.

Now I can tell you why so many people cannot receive healing. All the promises are potentially—not literally—yours. Never simply pick a promise out of God's Word and say, "Oh, this is mine; I will repeat it over and over again. This is mine, this is mine!" NO! It is potentially yours, yes, but make it yours in practical reality by waiting upon the Lord.

Before the Lord quickens a scripture to an individual, the Lord has many things to do. The Lord wants to cleanse your life and make you surrendered to Him, The Lord will never give promises promiscuously. As the Lord deals with you, take time to wait upon Him; confessing your sins, and surrendering your life to Him. When these conditions are met, then the power of God comes. Your heart—like the pool of Bethesda—is troubled by a particular scripture; and you know that its promise is yours, and you have the faith to bring about the needed miracle.

God's Uppermost Goal

The healing of the physical body is not the Spirit's

ultimate goal. You must know where the priority lies. His ultimate goal is the healing of our souls. When God deals with you, He always deals with you through the healing of your soul. If your soul is not right with God, no amount of prayer, shouting or jumping will bring the *rhema* of healing to you.

You must first get right with the Lord. Confess your sins, apply the blood of Jesus Christ, be saved and receive eternal life; then the Holy Spirit is going to prick your heart with a scripture of divine healing, inspire you, and give you the *rhema* you need. But in order for this to happen, you must wait on the Lord.

Divine healing is all according to God's sovereign will. Sometimes a person receives healing instantly; another person must wait a longer time.

One of our church's finest deacons became ill; this deacon gave everything to the Lord, loving God, and working for the Lord in an amazing way. He was told that he had a growth inside his body and that the doctor wanted to operate. But everybody in my church knew that God was going to heal him, for he was a tremendous saint with great faith. This was their reasoning.

I prayed for his healing. All of our then 40,000 members prayed, storming the Throne of Grace. And that deacon claimed the healing.

But nothing happened. He became worse and worse.

Eventually he bled so badly he was carried to the hospital and operated on. Many of my members were worried, and they complained, "Where is God? Why is God treating him like this?"

But I praised God, for I knew that He had some specific purpose in what was happening.

When he was hospitalized in the ward he began to preach the Gospel to all the people with whom he made contact. Soon the whole hospital knew that there was a living Jesus, His representative right in their hospital. The doctors, nurses, and all the patients daily became saved.

Then our members rejoiced, saying, "Praise God. It was far better for him to be in the hospital than to be divinely healed immediately."

God showed that His priority was the eternal healing of souls rather than the earthly healing of the physical.

When there is pain and suffering, we are apt to claim deliverance. But this we should not do. If your suffering should bring about redemptive grace, or if your suffering becomes the channel for the flowing of God's redeeming grace, then your suffering has been God-appointed. If, however, your suffering becomes invalid and starts to destroy you, then this is from satan, and you should pray through and rid yourself of it.

I will relay to you one case in which God did not

deliver people from their suffering.

It was during the Korean War when 500 ministers were captured and immediately shot to death, and two thousand churches were destroyed.

The Communists were vicious to the ministers. One minister's family was captured in Inchon, Korea, and the Communist leaders put them on what they called a 'People's Trial.' The accusers would say, "One man is guilty of causing this kind of sin, and for that kind of sin it is proper that he be punished."

The only response then given would be a chorus of voices agreeing, "Yah, Yah!"

This time they dug a large hole, putting the pastor, his wife, and several of his children in. The leader then spoke, "Mister, all these years you misled the people with the superstition of the Bible. Now if you will publicly disclaim it before these people, and repent of this misdemeanor, then you, your wife, and your children will be freed. But if you persist in your superstitions, all of your family is going to be buried alive. Make a decision!"

All of his children then blurted, "Oh Daddy! Daddy! Think of us! Daddy!"

Think of it. If you were in his place, what would you do? I am the father of three children, and would almost feel like going to hell rather than see my children killed.

This father was shaken. He lifted up his hand and said, "Yes, yes, I'll do it. I am going to denounce... my..."

But before he could finish his sentence his wife nudged him, saying, "Daddy! Say NO!"

"Hush children," she said. "Tonight we are going to have supper with the King of kings, the Lord of lords!"

She led them in singing 'In the Sweet By and By,' her husband and children following, while the Communists began to bury them. Soon the children were buried, but until the soil came up to their necks they sang, and all the people watched. God did not deliver them, but almost all of those people who watched this execution became Christians, many now members of my church.

Through their suffering the grace of redemption flowed. God gave His only begotten Son to be crucified on the cross so that this world could be saved and redeemed. That is God's uppermost goal – the redemption of souls. So when you desire divine healing, or an answer from above, always focus through the lenses of the uppermost goal, the redeeming of souls. If you see that your suffering brings about more redemption than your healing, then do not ask for deliverance, but ask God to give you strength to persevere.

To discern between suffering brought by satan that

God would rather deliver, and suffering that God would use to bring about the flow of redemptive grace, is not always easy. To make this kind of decision you need to wait upon the Lord, and to know the will of the Lord. Do not become discouraged, and go around receiving prayer from one famous evangelist and then another. But through your prayer, fasting and faith, let God show you His will.

When the Holy Spirit quickens the *logos* of scripture to you, a miraculous faith is imparted to your heart. You know that the scripture no longer belongs to the "said word" of God, but is instantly the "saying word" of God for you. You must then stand upon that word, and go ahead and do it, even though you can see nothing. Even though you cannot touch anything and even though your whole life is pitch dark, once you receive the *rhema* do not be frightened. Just go ahead and walk on the water, and you will see a miracle. Be careful, however, not to move ahead of God.

Many people do move ahead of God, even as did Paul, in his eagerness to bring the Gospel of Jesus Christ. Jesus Christ had commanded that we go to the ends of the world and preach the Gospel; so Paul went out on the *logos,* and headed for Asia. But the Spirit of Jesus Christ did not permit him to go there.

Then Paul said, "I will go to Bithynia." But again

the Spirit of the Lord said "NO."

Paul and his company then went down to Troas, an unknown city. We can imagine his wonderings there, that he was confused, thinking to himself, "I was just obeying the command of Jesus. Jesus said to go to the ends of the world and preach the Gospel. Why am I a failure?"

But as he was praying and waiting upon the Lord, he received the *rhema,* and a man from Macedonia appeared in a vision and said, "Come into Macedonia and help us!" So he took a boat and crossed over to Europe.

Through Paul's example we can again see the difference between *logos* and *rhema.*

Receiving Rhema

People have come to me and commented, "Brother Cho, I can pray through about the various promises from the scriptures, and I can wait until the Holy Spirit quickens and applies them to me. But how can I get *rhema* about choosing a husband, or a wife? I read all the scriptures, but the Bible does not say whether I should go marry Elizabeth, Mary or Joan. How can I get the *rhema* about this?

"Also, the Bible does not say that you should go and live in Lakeland, Los Angeles, or in some northern area. How can I receive God's will about that?"

These are legitimate questions. Let me show you the five steps I use to get the *rhema* about these types of decisions.

Neutral Gear

The first step is to put myself in neutral gear – not forward or backward, but completely calm in my heart. Then I wait upon the Lord, saying, "Lord, I'm here. I will listen to your voice. If you say 'yes,' I will go; if you say 'no,' I'm not going. I don't wish to make decisions for my own benefit, but to decide according to Your desire. Whether it becomes good for me, or bad for me, I'm ready to accept your guidance."

With this attitude I wait upon the Lord. Many times the best action to take is to fast and pray, for if you eat too much you get so tired that you cannot pray. Then, if you know that you are really calmed down, you come to the second step.

Divine Desire

The second thing I do is to ask the Lord to reveal His will through my desire. God always comes to you through your sanctified desire. "Delight thyself also in the Lord; and He shall give thee the desires of thine heart" (Psalm 37:4). "The desire of the righteous shall be granted" (Proverbs 10:24). "What things soever ye desire, when ye pray, believe that ye receive them, and ye shall have them" (Mark 11:24).

Desire, then, is one of God's focusing points. Moreover, Philippians 2:13 reads, "For it is God which worketh in you, both to will and to do of His good pleasure."

Through the Holy Spirit God puts in your heart the desire, making you to will to do His will. So pray to the Lord, "Lord, now give me the desire according to your will."

Pray through and wait upon the Lord until God gives you divine desire. As you pray many desires, beautiful desires, will probably flow in. In your praying, then, also have the patience to wait for God's desire to settle in. Do not stand up and say, "Oh, I've got everything," and rush away. Wait upon the Lord a little longer. Desires can be given from satan, from your own spirit, or from the Holy Spirit.

Time is always the test. If you wait patiently your own desire and desires from satan will become increasingly weaker, but the desire from the Holy Spirit becomes stronger and stronger. So wait, and receive the divine desire.

Scriptural Screening

After my desire becomes very clear-cut, then I proceed to step three: I compare this desire with Biblical teaching.

One day a lady came to me. All excited, she said, "Oh, Pastor Cho, I am going to support your ministry with a large amount of money."

"Praise God," I exclaimed. "Have a seat and tell me about this."

She explained, "I have a fantastic desire to go into business. This business deal is going on, and if I join in I think I can make big money."

"What kind of business is it?" I asked.

She replied, "I have a burning desire to get a monopoly on the cigarette business. Tobacco, you know."

"Forget about it," I retorted.

"But I have the desire!" she said. "The burning desire, just like you've preached about."

"That desire is from your own flesh," I replied. "Have you ever gone through the Bible to see if what you would be doing is scriptural?"

"No,"

"Your desire must be screened through the scripture," I instructed her. "The Bible says that you are the temple of the Holy Spirit (1 Corinthians 6:19). If God ever wanted His people to smoke, then He would have made our noses differently. Smoke stacks are supposed to be open upward to the sky, and not downward. Think about the nose; it is not pointing upward, but downward. God did not purpose that people smoke, because our smoke stacks are upside down. The Holy Spirit's dwelling is your body. If you pollute it with smoke, then you are polluting the temple of the Holy Spirit with smoke. Your desire is out of the will of God. It would be best if you just forget about this new business."

One man came to me and said, "Pastor, I've struck up a friendship with a beautiful woman, a widow. She is sweet, beautiful and wonderful, and when I pray, I have a burning desire to marry her. But I also have my wife and children."

"Look," I replied, "you forget about this, because it's from the devil."

"Oh, no, no. This is not from the devil," he disagreed. "When I prayed the Holy Spirit spoke in my heart and told me that my original wife was not exactly the right kind of rib to fit into my side. My present wife is always a thorn in my flesh. The Holy Spirit spoke and said that this widow is my lost rib, which will fit exactly into my side."

I told him, "That is not from the Holy Spirit. That's

from the devil's spirit."

Many people make this kind of mistake. If they pray against the written Word of God, then the devil will speak. The Holy Spirit will never contradict God's written Word. That man did not listen to me, and he divorced his wife and he married that widow. He is now of all men the most miserable. He found out that his second rib was even worse than his first.

So all of our desires should be carefully screened with Scripture. If you do not have the self-confidence to do this yourself, then go to your minister or pastor.

A Beckoning Signal

After I screen my desire through the written Word, the teachings of God, then I am ready for step four: to ask God for a beckoning signal from my circumstances. If God truly has spoken to your heart, then He is bound to give you a signal from the outside external world.

When Elijah prayed seven times for rain, he received a signal from the eastern sky—a patch as large as a man's fist, a cloud, appeared.

Gideon also provides us with an example, for he, too, asked for a sign. And God would always show me a sign from my circumstances; sometimes this sign was very small, but it still was a sign.

Divine Timing

After I have received a sign, then I take the final step: I pray until I know God's timing. God's timing is different from our timing.

You must pray—until you have a real peace, for peace is like the chief umpire. If after you pray you still feel a restlessness in your spirit, then the timing is not proper. That means there is still a red light; so keep praying and waiting. When the red light is switched off and you see the green light, peace will come into your heart.

Then you should jump up and go. Go then with full speed, with God's blessing and God's *rhema*. Miracle after miracle will follow you.

All through life I have carried out and conducted my business by using these five steps. So far God has always confirmed this way of walking with signs and miracles following. These results must show clearly the difference between *logos* and *rhema*.

In the future you need no longer be confused about the promises of God. No amount of claiming, travailing, jumping, or shrieking will convince Him. God is going to convince you Himself by imparting His faith into your heart.

The English translation of Mark 11:22–23 says that

you should have faith in God and then you would be able to command a mountain to be removed and cast into the sea. The Greek, however, says that you should have the faith *of* God.

How can you have the faith *of* God? When you receive *rhema* the faith given is not your own; it is imparted faith that God has given you. After receiving this imparted faith, then you can command mountains to be removed. Without receiving God's faith you cannot do this.

If for no other reason, you should carefully study the Bible—Genesis to Revelation—in order to give the Holy Spirit the material with which He needs to work. Then when you wait upon the Lord, the Holy Spirit will impart His faith to you. Great miracles will follow you as you act on this faith, miracles in your ministry and in your home.

So wait upon the Lord; never consider it a waste of time. When God speaks to your heart He can in one second do far greater things than you could do in one entire year. Wait upon the Lord, and you will see great things accomplished.

5

THE SCHOOL OF ANDREW

When you receive Jesus Christ as your personal Saviour your spirit is instantly reborn. Right away God's life is poured into you, and instantly your spiritual being receives eternal life. But your mind, your thoughts, must be renewed according to your born again spirit; that task of renewal is one that requires a lifelong process, taking time, energy and struggle, This renewal is necessary if one is to adequately receive and act on the *rhema* they are given from God, allowing the powerful creativity of the spoken word to remain vital.

A Renewed Thought Life

Many people experience a spiritual rebirth, but they do not renew their mind in order to truly grasp the thoughts of God. They do not align their personal lives according to the thoughts of God. For this reason God, who dwells in them, cannot freely move through the channel of their thinking life. Let me illustrate this more clearly.

One day my eldest son, who at that time was in fourth grade, came to me. I could tell he wanted to ask me something, but he was hesitant in speaking. Finally I spoke first: "Son, what are you trying to ask me?"

He smiled. "Daddy, if I ask you a strange question, will you get mad?"

"Of course I won't get mad," I assured him. "Go ahead. Speak."

"Well," he continued, "are you permitted to tell a lie before your own congregation?"

"When did I tell a lie?" I asked.

He laughed, "I've heard you telling a lie again and again to your congregation."

I was shocked. If my son distrusted me, then who could trust me? "Son," I said, "you sit down and tell me when I told a lie."

"Daddy, so many times you told your congregation that you had heard from the Lord, so I became curious. Every Saturday I would listen outside your study as you were preparing your sermons, and I would open the door a little to see if you were really meeting God there.

"But I never saw you really meeting God in your study. Yet on Sunday you come out to the platform and boldly declare to the people that you've met God. And that's a lie, isn't it? Don't be afraid of telling me the truth. I am your son. I won't tell the people."

Since he was so young I knew that he would not understand if I were to explain my feelings in theological terms. "Lord," I prayed, "you must give me wisdom. How can I explain to this young mind my relationship with you?"

Suddenly a tremendous thought flowed out of my heart, and I looked at my son and said, "Son, let me ask you a question. Have you ever seen your thoughts?"

He paused a moment. "No, I haven't seen my thoughts."

"Then you have an empty head," I answered. "You have no thoughts at all."

"No, Daddy, I do have thoughts. Because I have thoughts I can talk."

"But," I pointed out, "I haven't seen your thoughts."

"How can you see my thoughts?" he asked. "They are somewhere in my brain, and you can't see them."

"Well, then," I said, "even though you can't see them you really have thoughts, don't you?"

"Sure, Daddy," he answered.

"Well," I explained, "I meet God even though you can't see Him with your eyes. God is like your thoughts. The Bible says that God is the Word.

"Son, what is the Word? The Word is thought clothed with vocabulary. And if God is thought clothed with Chinese, the Chinese people understand God's thoughts; when God's thoughts are clothed with English, then American people understand. When God's thoughts come down to us clothed in the Korean language we Korean people understand.

"Son, I meet God by reading the Scripture, the Word of God; and God's thoughts touch my thoughts in an unseen realm, and I have conversation with the Heavenly Father through the Word of God. God is like thought."

Immediately my son caught the meaning, and he nodded. "I can't see my thoughts, but I still know that I have them. Yes, God is like thought. I can't see God, but God is there. I am satisfied. I am sorry, Father, because I misunderstood you."

When my son left I stood up and praised the Lord: "Father, I was afraid that he would not understand, but he did; yet I know it was not I, but the Holy Spirit who helped me to have the words to explain your wonderful presence."

Now let me ask you a question. What is God like? Does God have any forms? Does He look like a human being? How can you explain the presence of God?

God is like thought. If you do not have any thoughts, then God has no channel through which to speak to you. You cannot touch God with your hands, you cannot breathe God as if breathing air into your lungs; for God does not belong to the sensual world. You can meet God only through the arena of your thinking life.

God's thoughts come through His Word, or through His Holy Spirit. His thoughts touch your thoughts, and it is there that you meet God. So if you do not renew your thinking life and if you do not renew your mind after conversion, then God cannot really manifest Himself to you.

Many people still live with their old minds after conversion. This old way of thinking is limiting; thus God becomes limited by the wrong kind of thinking life. To walk closely with God you must renew your mind and your thinking life. If you do not renew your thinking life, God cannot come and commune with you. God will not dwell in a polluted mind, as fish and birds will not remain in a polluted lake.

You must renew your thinking in order that faith can rise up through your thinking life. Faith does not just well up from your inner spirit. Faith comes in cooperation with your thoughts, for faith comes by hearing, and hearing by the Word of God.

First you must hear; and through hearing, the Word of God comes to your thoughts; through your thinking life, the thoughts of God go into your spirit and produce faith. Therefore, if you do not renew your thinking, you cannot fully understand the Word of God; and without the renewal of mind and the hearing of the Word, you cannot have faith. Faith comes by hearing.

And what do you hear? You hear the thoughts of God. The arena of your thinking engrafts God's thoughts and produces faith, and through faith God can flow through you to others. Your thinking life is so important; you must renew your mind. There are three steps by which you can renew your mind, and these three steps must be followed before you can achieve a renewal of your thought life.

A Changed Thinking Attitude

Your first step must be to change your thinking attitude from that of a negative attitude to that of a positive one. Let us look at Peter, Jesus Christ's disciple, as an example.

The disciples of Jesus Christ were in a boat on the Sea of Galilee. It was a dark and stormy night, and the waves were so high that the boat rolled heavily. They were fighting a losing battle to keep the boat afloat when suddenly they saw Jesus Christ walking on the water toward them. In those days there was a popular saying that if a seaman saw a ghost on the sea his boat would sink. So when these fishermen-disciples saw Christ they were frozen with fear, thinking that their boat was going to sink and that they were going to die.

But Jesus spoke, "I am Christ. Don't be frightened."

Peter cried out, "If you were Jesus, you would ask me to come to you."

Peter always spoke before he thought. He was a

terribly emotional man; but he had the gift of boldness, so God used him.

Christ then told Peter to come. When Peter heard this command, he immediately accepted the command of Jesus in his mind, and his thinking was renewed.

Humanly speaking, Peter could never walk on the water, but when he accepted the word of Jesus Christ, he instantly renewed his mind. Peter changed his thinking from a negative to a positive attitude. Peter would never have believed that he could walk on water, but as he heard the command of Jesus and as he accepted the command, he changed his thoughts; he believed that he could walk on water. He changed his thinking, and man always acts according to his thoughts.

So as Peter renewed his thoughts, as he envisioned that he could walk on water, he acted accordingly, and he jumped out of the boat. It was a pitch dark night, and the waves were high. But he risked his life boldly, launching out by faith, and began to walk on the water.

Miracles follow a renewed mind, and as Peter renewed his mind, he began to walk on water. He walked high on the crest of the waves; he was actually walking on water!

But suddenly he looked around. He saw the dark valleys the stormy waves created, and he began to regress into his old thinking. "Look at me," he thought.

"Am I not a human being? I am walking on the water, and we are not supposed to be able to walk like this. We human beings are supposed to walk on land, not on water. I'm not a fish, but look at me. I'm walking on the water. This is wrong; it's impossible for me to do this."

He changed his thinking pattern. He thought that he could not walk on the water, and instantly he sank.

God relates to each of us only through our thought life. When Peter received the *rhema* from Christ, renewed his thinking and therefore thought he could walk on the water, he walked. When he changed this thinking and thought it impossible to walk on the water, he instantly began to sink.

This is a very important concept, for as a man thinketh, so will he act. If you think you are a king or queen, you will act like a king or queen. If you think of yourself as being unworthy and of no account, then you will behave as if you are unworthy and of no account.

So it is vital that we renew our thoughts, and think positively. Let me illustrate this point with an actual example.

I once knew a doctor who claimed to be an atheist. I suffered much because of him; for a long time he was a great enemy to my ministry, challenging my faith, attacking my words and beliefs.

Then one day that doctor suffered a stroke and became paralysed. As a result of his paralysis, he was slowly dying. The doctor then came to my church, asking that I pray for his healing.

Many people brag about their atheistic views; yet when these same people experience a pitch dark night, and encounter the storm tossed waves, their atheism becomes very weak.

So this doctor came to the church, and I prayed for him. He received the prayer of faith, and he stood up and walked from his wheelchair, his steps strong. All the people clapped their hands and shouted, praising God.

Next Sunday he came to the church, walking by himself with no assistance. He again requested my personal prayer, but as I was busy I could not. When he saw that I could not personally pray for him, he changed his thinking; his thoughts regressed, and he returned into his old self. Because he could not receive the prayer of faith from me, he became unbelieving again, and as he walked out of my office to his car, he collapsed, and his wife had to call an ambulance to carry him to the hospital.

He collapsed because he changed his thoughts. The power of God left him, and just as Peter began to doubt and sink into the Sea of Galilee, so did the doctor lose himself to his fears, and again become paralysed.

Thoughts are important, so do not neglect to renew your thinking life. Be absolutely positive in your thinking. Do not think negatively. God is light, and in Him there is no darkness; there is nothing negative in God, for in God there is only the positive. Positive things are happenings; so to commune with God you must renew your mind to think positively. Feed your mind with Scripture, for the Word of God is full of positive life.

Also, be careful when you feed on the Word of God that you do not confine your thinking to traditional patterns of thought.

Be revolutionary. Many people are bound because they think only in the traditional, orthodox way, and therefore God is unable to accomplish the great works He desires to accomplish through them. But if you receive the Word of God and revolutionize your thinking, then you will achieve heights beyond your present limitations.

When I am in Korea I have a session with my one hundred associate pastors every morning. Each morning, from 9:00 to 9:30 a.m., I challenge them, asking them to revolutionize their thinking.

"'Don't just think traditionally," I exhort them. "Don't go by the thinking and teaching of Cho. Go by the Word of God. Feed on the Word of God. Revolutionize your thinking life! Expand your thinking life according to Scripture; then God can have absolute freedom to express Himself through your thoughts."

After I speak these words those associates become increasingly motivated. They receive the Word, and if they hit a real revolutionary thought, they carry it out, and then I see the results. I do not intervene with their work, except for those occasions when they experience difficulty.

Once I have delegated power, that power remains delegated, and I no longer worry about it. It is through this positive approach that I work with my associates, successful ministers, each responsible for meeting the needs of a certain portion of a 50,000 adult membership.

Think in Terms of Miracles

When you have changed your thinking attitude from that of a negative attitude to that of a positive one, your second step must be to constantly train yourself to think in terms of miracles. This can be seen in the lives of the disciples of Jesus Christ.

Once Jesus went out to the wilderness with 5,000 men following him. Besides 5,000 men there were probably 10,000 women, women who also had children; in actuality then, there was probably a total of 20,000 in this crowd. As evening approached the people became hungry. It was getting dark and cold, and the women and children began falling back along the side of the road.

Christ called Philip, "Philip, I can see all these folks are hungry. Feed them."

So Philip received the command from the Lord Jesus Christ to feed this large crowd. To transfer what happened in modern terms, can't you see Philip organizing what would be today a committee, in order to study how to feed this large number of people? Imagine him recruiting the members of his committee, calling together disciples with a high intelligence.

Philip opened the committee meeting as chairman, saying, "Gentlemen, our Lord Jesus Christ commanded me to feed these 20,000 people in the wilderness. So our committee has the responsibility to find the way to do so. Do you have any ideas?"

One fellow lifted his hand, and after Philip recognized him, said, "Don't you know that we are in the wilderness? We aren't in downtown Jerusalem. It's absolutely impossible to even think of feeding these people."

"I think so, too," Philip might have answered.

"Mister Scribe, write that down."

A second man lifted his hand, "Mr. Chairman, I want to ask you a question. Do we have enough money? We would need at least two hundred denarii to feed even a small portion of them. Do we have enough money?"

"No," Philip responded, "we haven't got a penny."

"Well, you are out of your mind trying to feed them then," the man retorted.

"Yes, I agree with you," Philip returned. "Mr. Scribe, write that down, also."

A third man spoke: "Mr. Chairman, do you know any bakery that could produce so much bread at one time?"

"No," said Philip, "I don't know any bakery around here."

"Well then, it'd take weeks to feed these people, and that's impossible!"

"Yes, I agree with you," said Philip. "Mr. Scribe, write that down, too."

Then another disciple spoke, "I want to express my opinion, too, Mr. Chairman. You know it's getting late. Why don't we just scatter them and tell them to each find a place to sleep and eat?"

The meeting was then concluded, and Philip gathered the information. But this information was only of a negative and impossibility nature, information that refuted the teachings of Jesus Christ, and directly opposed His command.

Philip then went to Jesus to inform Him, but as he began to speak, Andrew walked up with five loaves of bread, and two fishes in his hand. "Andrew," Philip exclaimed, "are you trying to make fun of us? What are you doing? You have five loaves of bread and two fishes to feed 20,000 people! You are really out of your mind!"

But Andrew did not answer him. He just brought the five loaves and two fishes to Jesus.

"Jesus, this isn't enough to feed many people, but I brought it here anyway."

Andrew heard the command of Jesus; his mind accepted the command, and though he doubted, he brought the food he found to Christ. Andrew had possibility thinking, and through his thinking, caught the vision of Jesus Christ.

Then Jesus blessed that bread and fishes, multiplied them, and that great crowd was fed.

All Christians belong to Jesus Christ; but in Christ there are two schools of thought: Philip's school and Andrew's school. Unfortunately, many churches belong to the school of Philip, only talking about the impossible. They cry that this is the wilderness and that it is too late, and that the people cannot be fed. They speak with little faith, and talk only of the impossible.

To what school do you belong? I know that many attend different schools and colleges, but what school do you belong to in your thinking life? Do you belong to Philip's school, or do you belong to the school of Andrew?

When God spoke to my heart in 1969, and told me to build a church that would seat 10,000 people, I was frightened. Every moment I felt like Philip. I talked with the board of elders, and all of them thought like the disciples of Philip. They would tell me it was impossible.

When I talked with my 600 deacons, again I found every one of them thinking the same way. So I, too, joined the school of Philip, and I came to Jesus and told Him I could not build that church. But in my heart Christ commanded me, "I did not ask you to confer with your deacons and elders. I told you to go and build."

"Lord," I replied, "you know that I don't have anything to build with. It will take so much more money than I have now."

Then through the Holy Spirit Jesus spoke to my heart, "What do you have that you personally could give?"

In my heart I knew what He was asking, but I refused to recognize His request, saying, "Jesus, don't ask me to do that. I married when I was thirty years old, and throughout the years I've saved my money so that I could build a beautiful home and give it to my wife. I can't sell that house."

But the Lord replied, "Give what you have."

"Father, it's just $20,000," I cried. "That can't build the church and apartment complex. They cost $5 million. The amount my house would bring could not possibly be enough."

But God said, "Sell your home and bring that money to me with faith."

"Oh, God, this is terrible!" I responded. "How can I do that?"

"If you are ever to believe my Word," the Lord admonished me, "you must first be willing to give of what you have and what you own."

To a Korean wife the home is everything. It is the place she raises her children, it is the place she builds her life, it is a precious possession to her. So I was afraid to tell my wife, and I began to travail in prayer. I prayed that my wife would consent about the selling of our home.

That evening I bought gifts of flowers and scarves home to my wife. "Why are you bringing me these gifts?" she asked. "Are you worried that I don't love you any more?" But she was pleased, and she fixed the evening meal happily.

"Oh, praise God," I responded. "I'm so happy that I've chosen you. If God ever wanted me to choose another girl again, I'd still pick you. You are more beautiful to me each day." After a time, when I felt the moment to be right, I said, "Honey, I have a big problem."

Concerned, she looked at me, insisting, "Tell me."

"We are going to build this big church which will seat 10,000 people," I told her. "It will cost five million dollars and as I was praying about this matter, the Holy Spirit spoke to my heart and said that if I was to get the money for the church, I would have to start from my own household. God wants us to submit five loaves of bread and two fishes...and those five loaves and two fishes are our house!"

My wife turned pale, and then looking straight into my eyes she said, "This home is mine, not yours. Don't you dare touch this house. It belongs to me and to my children. You cannot give this house up."

Her reaction was just as I had feared. Then I went to the Lord and prayed, "Lord, now I've done what I can. The rest is up to you. Send your Holy Spirit to prick her heart, so that she will surrender."

That night as I prayed, I could see my wife constantly turning and tossing in her sleep. I knew then that the

Holy Spirit was working. I said to the Lord, "Oh, God, keep on nudging her."

And sure enough, the Lord nudged her; for almost a week she could not sleep, and her eyes became bloodshot. Finally she came to me, "I cannot stand it any longer. I cannot refuse what the Holy Spirit wants. I'll give up the house." So she brought the title deed for the house, and together we took that title deed and gave our home for the construction of the church. We were like Andrew, who though he had only five loaves and two fishes in his hand, had the faith that Jesus could take this small portion of food and feed an entire crowd. We, too, belonged to the school of Andrew.

One day, however, a problem about the land we planned to build on came up. The Korean government was developing a special piece of land called Yoido Island. This piece of property was going to be modeled after New York's Manhattan Island. They were building government buildings on the land and would allow only one church there. Church bids came from all over Korea: the Presbyterian, Methodist, Baptist, Catholic, Buddhist and Confucists applied to the government. All were screened and passed through Congress for permission to build a church on this special land.

I also submitted an application. The man in charge

looked at me and asked, "What denomination do you belong to?"

"The Assemblies of God," I replied.

"You mean that church where they shout praises to God in such a loud and noisy way? And pray for the sick and speak in strange tongues?"

"That's right," I responded.

He shook his head, "You know this church is going to be right in front of the new Congress Hall. This church has got to be dignified, and your church is not. We can't accept your application."

I was happy in my heart, however, because this would excuse me from building the church. I returned to the Lord in prayer, "Lord, you heard that, didn't you? We are not dignified enough to build there."

You can bring every excuse you can think of to the Lord, but the Holy Spirit always has the answer. The Holy Spirit responded, saying, "When did I ask you to go and apply for a building permit?"

"Am I not supposed to?" I questioned.

"My child," He answered, "you should not follow the path you are now walking. You must walk the other way, the way of prayer and faith."

So I began to fast and pray. Then in my heart the wisdom of the Holy Spirit spoke, "Go and find who is in charge of developing that island."

I went and soon found that the city's vice mayor was in charge of developing the whole area. I began to ask about his personal home and life, and I found out that his mother was a member of a Presbyterian church. So I visited her, praying with her, and she became filled with the Holy Spirit. She then began to come to my church.

In Korea, the mother-in-law carries quite a bit of power and authority over the daughter-in-law. I told this woman to bring her daughter-in-law to church, telling her, "Your daughter-in-law has got to be saved."

So she prayed and I prayed, and she brought her son's wife to the church. After listening to the sermon she gave her heart to Christ and was filled with the Holy Spirit.

I then began to work through her, thinking to myself, "If I've got the wife, I know I can get to the husband." So I instructed her, "You've got to bring your husband to church."

"But he is so busy," she replied.

"You don't want him to go to hell, do you?" I sternly asked. "So bring him to church."

When eventually she brought him I preached a powerful message. Though I was not looking directly at his face, I was really preaching for him; and miraculously he gave his heart to the Lord.

The next Sunday he walked into my office. "Pastor, you know I'm in charge of the development of Yoido Island. We are permitting one Korean church to come and build there. I wish we could bring our church there."

I wanted to shout, but the Holy Spirit would not allow me to. Sometimes the Holy Spirit works in very mysterious ways; the Holy Spirit impressed my heart to say no, but I argued, "No. I've worked so hard for this." While my heart was crying to say yes, I replied, "No, Mr. Vice Mayor. To bring this church to Yoido would take an enormous amount of money, and we would have to buy at least three or four acres of land. That would cost more than five million dollars. I think it's impossible. To make matters worse, we are considered an undignified Pentecostal church, and they would not even accept my application."

He smiled and said, "I think I have a way. You pray for one week and then I'll come back. You can give me the answer then, because I can take care of it quickly."

For one week I prayed, and the next week he returned to my office. "Pastor, if you make the decision to move the church there, I'll make all the arrangements for you to have the choicest land. I'll also do all the paper work, with my own office paying the expenses. I'll send my man to Congress to get all the necessary agreements, and I'll do all the paper work for that, too. I'll do everything for you, and you will have the land. More than that, I'll make all the arrangements for you to buy the land by credit from the city government."

Then the Holy Spirit said in my heart, "SHOUT!"

"Mr. Vice Mayor," I said, "I accept."

God kept me from saying 'yes' for one week, and as a result we not only miraculously got the land, but were saved from doing all the paper work as well.

I then went and signed a contract with a construction company. Shortly afterwards they dug the foundation, and began the building of the church and apartment house complex. This Vice-Mayor is now one of the leading elders in my church.

In a similar way your faith is bound to be tested. If you have a small project, you will be tried in a small way; but if you have a big project, you will be tried in a big way. Never think that your faith will only travel through a field of roses. You will go through turbulence, by which God tests your faith.

So far in the building of the church I still belonged to the school of Andrew, and with great faith prayed through each new problem.

But then the dollar devaluation came, and the contractor broke the contract. He said they wanted to renegotiate, and he increased the cost of building the church. Then the oil crisis came, and all the banks closed. My people began to lose their jobs, and even with my total income per month, I could hardly meet even the interest on the loans. Not only could I not pay my staff in the church, but I received no salary myself.

Then the company began to sue me because I could not pay the necessary increase. I would come to the church, and notice after notice came, filing suit: the electric company, the sewage company, the construction company. Papers were piled on my desk, yet I had no money to pay any of them. I didn't even have the money to hire my own lawyer. I would sit behind my desk, and one by one the workers in my church began to leave because I could not give them their salaries. Nobody wants to stay in a sinking boat, and I was sinking fast.

Since we had sold our home and had no place to go, I brought my family to an unfinished apartment on the seventh floor of the unfinished apartment complex. There was no running water and no heat, and it was very cold.

Each evening I would come home to the barren apartment, and all night we would shiver in the cold weather. We had no food, and everything seemed so dark. I was hitting rock bottom, and fast becoming a disciple of Philip. I said to myself, "Yes, I made a mistake. I should never have believed God in such a way. I should have thought in the traditional pattern. I should not have started to walk on the water. All this business about faith is a fake. All those voices that I heard in my prayer life must have been the voices of my own consciousness, and not from the Holy Spirit. Yes, I made a mistake." And I began to feel sorry for myself.

People were beginning to leave my church, and all reports were negative; my family even began to doubt me. Everything seemed impossible, and I was tired and hungry. "This is it," I said. "This is the end. This is the so called life of faith. I am going to finish my life.

"I'm going to cast myself down," I continued. "I'm going to die. But I don't want to go to hell. I've been working for You all these years, and at least I should get something in return. If hell is worse than this place, why should I go there?

"But I can't live in the world like this. I am committing suicide, but please accept my soul and send me to heaven!"

The impact of prayer was more powerful than I realized, and as I prayed, I heard a voice saying, "You are a coward. You want to cast yourself down and become an object of ridicule for the people. Will you remain a coward? Or are you a man of faith?"

"Yes," I admitted, "I am a coward."

Again the voice spoke, "Not only will you go to hell, but you will also pull down many of your members who put their trust in you! You borrowed money from some of the elders and members. Remember the thousands of dollars you borrowed from the precious sisters in the church. They all put trust in you. And now you are throwing yourself down and committing suicide.

"You will cause a chain reaction. Because of your cowardice they will lose their faith. They will have broken homes, and some will also commit suicide. What a repercussion you will cause the Christian world to feel!"

These words poured into my heart. I slumped down, crying, "Oh, God, then what can I do? Why won't you let me die?"

God replied, "You cannot die, for you must persevere. You must see all the debts paid; all the people's debts must be cleared."

I stood up, left the seventh floor and went to my office. I knelt down, travailing and crying. News of my desperate state began to spread among the people. Suddenly they experienced a reawakening of faith, including those who had already left the church. "Let's save our preacher!" they cried. "Let's save the man of God!"

In this way a Save Our Pastor movement began. It was a cold winter, and we had no heat, but by the thousands the people began to flock into the ground floor of the unfinished church, thousands also fasting and praying through many nights. They cried and prayed, "Save the man of God. Save our Pastor!"

Then God began to move. Ladies would cut their long hair, bringing it to the platform to make wigs that could be sold. One day, in an especially moving scene, an eighty year old woman who had no children, no support, barely living by the help of the government, came to the platform, crying and trembling. She brought an old banged-up rice bowl, a pair of chopsticks and a spoon. As she stood there crying she said, "Pastor, I want to see you delivered from this situation. I want to see you helped, for your ministry was such a great blessing to me for so many years. I want to do something, but I have no money. This is all I have— this old rice bowl, a pair of chopsticks and a spoon. But I want to give it all to the Lord's work. I can eat out of cardboard, and I can eat with my fingers."

My heart was broken. "Lady," I said, "I can't accept this. It's all you have! You need these to eat your everyday meals. I can't accept it."

She broke down in tears, saying, "Wouldn't God accept this gift from an old dying woman? Wouldn't He? I know that this can't be of much help to you, but I want to give something."

Suddenly one businessman stood up and spoke, "Pastor, I want to buy that." And he paid nearly $30,000 just for that old banged-up bowl, chopsticks and spoon.

This began to light a fire. People began selling their good houses and moving to small apartments. There were young couples who gave their whole year's salary to the church, deciding to live by faith.

This great movement brought results, for soon money began to flow in, and I could pay the interest on the loan. Banks began to open their doors to me, and amazingly, in less than a year everything began to work out. I paid all the debts, and was cleared until 1973. Not only was I able to pay the interest, but I also had the five million dollars to finish building the church and apartment complex.

And God again proved that the school of Andrew is best, and that to think in terms of miracles is to think as God would have us think.

Many people think that when you have faith, everything will flow easily, with few problems encountered. But it is important to remember that this is not so.

Look at Abraham. He had faith, but he endured trials for 25 years; Jacob endured hardship for twenty years, Joseph for thirteen, Moses for forty, and the disciples of Christ passed through trials and temptations all their lives.

Do not be discouraged after going through a few weeks of difficulty or a few months of trial. Do not throw your hands up in defeat and cry, "Oh, where is God?"

God is always there, and He is testing you. Sometimes God wants to stiffen and strengthen your backbone; and sometimes while being strengthened you can almost hear the bones cracking. But if you stand on the Word of God and have faith, then God will never let you down. To illustrate this, I will relate another of my experiences.

I once wrote a $50,000 post-dated check, payable December 31. I scraped money from every source available, but I was unable to gather even a small portion of the amount. If I could not put the money in the bank by the designated day, the newspapers would carry headlines saying that the pastor of the largest church in Korea wrote a hot check.

It was twelve noon of the day the money had to be in, and I was praying, "Oh, God, I've spent all my money, more than I had. I've borrowed money from many people. Father, where will I go? I've no place to go."

I continued praying. Then the clock struck one o'clock, then two o'clock, then three o'clock. My wife then called, "Honey, did you get the money yet?"

"No," I answered.

She said, "Don't you know that at four o'clock the last plane pulls out of Seoul? That's your chance to escape to America."

"I can't do that. I can't avoid my responsibilities," I told her, "I can't escape. And if I did, a smear would come to the name of Jesus Christ. I'd rather meet whatever happens here in Korea than to escape the country."

The bank was to close at six o'clock, and it was now five. I became desperate. I could not sit, and I could not stand; I just walked and walked, back and forth, like a lion in a cage. Again I prayed, "Oh, God, please come and help me."

Suddenly the Holy Spirit let a thought flow through my mind. This thought was that I should go to the head of my bank and boldly ask him to write me a $50,000 check. "Father!" I responded. "I must be losing my mind. I've heated my mind's computer, and now it's become overloaded. I don't have anything to put up for mortgage. I have no paper work done. You want me to just go and ask him to write a $50,000 check? This is absolutely out of order!"

But the Holy Spirit insisted, "Yes, I do those things which are out of man's perceived natural order. You go and do it."

I called in my treasurer, "Mr. Park, would you go to the bank with me? I am going to ask the president of the bank to write me a $50,000 check."

He looked at me, then he began laughing, "You have really lost your mind, haven't you? This is December 31. It's five o'clock, you have no appointment, and people are lined up to see him.

"Moreover, we don't have any assets for collateral. No paper work has been done. It's foolish. I'm not going with you. If you want to go, go ahead; but I don't want to be a fool with you."

"Okay," I returned. "I am going with a renewed mind, whereas you are confined by a traditional mind."

I took the car and rushed to the bank. The parking lot was packed, but I managed to park, and I walked into the bank.

Humanly speaking, there was no way for me to meet the president. His secretary's office was filled with people. "Dear Holy Spirit," I said, "I've come this far. Please give me more instructions."

The Holy Spirit answered, "Walk courageously. Be

very bold. Act like a big shot. Don't pay any attention to anyone else, but just walk straight through to the president's office."

So I straightened up, walking through. His secretary noticed me and asked, "Sir, where are you going?"

I looked right into her eyes, but said nothing. She again questioned, "Sir, who are you? Have you an appointment? Who are you?"

Suddenly an inspiration came to me. "I am from the highest authority," I responded. I meant I was sent from God, but she thought that I had been sent from the President of Korea, for in Korea the President is the highest authority. Thinking that I was a special emissary from the President, her attitude changed. She became polite, and ready to please. "You're from the highest authority?" she asked. "Yes, you may meet him." Then turning to the people waiting she said, "This man must go ahead."

She took me ahead of everyone else, straight through to the bank president's office. As I walked in I said, "Dear Holy Spirit, now I've gotten this far. What can I do now?" The Spirit of the Lord was upon me, and just as He had come upon other men of faith, I was made bold.

The Spirit kept repeating, "You are a child of the King, an important person. Keep acting like the big shot you are." So I boldly walked in, sat on the sofa, and crossed my legs.

The president walked in, greeting me with a big smile, and extending his hand asked, "What kind of business do you have? For what purpose did you come? Do I know you?" I did not answer his questions, but instead said, "Sir, I've come here with a tremendous project, and I am going to do a great favor for you."

"A favor?" he queried.

"If you do a small favor for me, then I will give you 10,000 new banking accounts the beginning of this new year," I told him.

"Ten thousand new bank accounts!" he exclaimed.

"Pick up the phone and call the police. Ask about the name Yonggi Cho, and you'll find that he is the pastor of the largest church in Seoul. He has more than 10,000 members, and also has great authority over his Christians. He can have all of them transfer their bank account to your bank for the new year. I will do this tremendous favor for you if you do one for me."

He called his secretary right away to check what I said. All the facts cleared as true. He then asked, "What is this favor I could do for you?"

"You write me a $50,000 check," I told him. "I have no time to do all the legal paper work. But you are a businessman. I am the King's Businessman. Many times a businessman enters a huge undertaking with nothing but faith and confidence to show that he will succeed. Small business matters need to go through the law and paper work, but when we make a big deal, we bypass these things and trust that the deal will be successful. If you are a big businessman – and I think that you are – then you will do this for me."

The president called in his vice-president, and the vice-president said, "You can't do that. Your neck would really be on the line. It's not just $5,000. It's $50,000, and he has no collateral, no papers. You can't do it."

"If you won't do it," I interjected, "then I have other places I could go. I could do this favor for the Cho Heung Bank.

The man sat down and shook his head. Then he said, "Sir, I feel funny. I've never felt this kind of emotion before in my life. I trust you. If I didn't trust you so much I would never do this. But I kind of like you; you are a bold person, and I like your faith. I'll be putting my whole career and life in your hands by doing this, and after this I'll never do it again; but this time I'll stick my neck out. Bring me a $50,000 check," he instructed his vice-president. "I trust you to keep your promise," he told me as he wrote out a check for $50,000 from his own personal savings.

As I walked out of the office with the check, I felt ten feet tall. Once again I was in the school of Andrew. I turned in the money just as the bank was closing at six o'clock, and I was saved.

Many times God waits until the last moment. Once you renew your mind and once you learn how to walk with God, then you must persist to the last moment. Do not be frightened.

Renew your thinking life. Do not be confined by traditional thinking, but study the Word of God. This is the textbook with which you can renew your mind, and fill your mind with positive thinking, and learn to think in terms of miracles.

Orient Your Mind to God's Success

The third step to a renewed mind is a mind filled with an orientation to success. You must permeate your mind with a victory consciousness, and an abundance consciousness. God never fails. So if it is God's thoughts you are receiving, you will always be successful.

God never loses a war, for He is the eternal victor; you should have victory consciousness. God never lacks for anything; you should have abundance consciousness.

This consciousness is important. If you have inferiority consciousness, poverty consciousness, sickness consciousness, or failure consciousness, God can never work.

God is your help, God is your abundance, God is your success, and God is your victory. If two men do not agree, how can they work together? So to walk and work with God, you must engraft God's types of consciousness to your own.

Renew your mind. Constantly think in terms of success, in terms of victory, and in terms of abundance. When you have completely renewed your thinking process, then you will receive the *rhema* of God. Boldly assimilate the Word of God into your thinking life. Through prayer produce faith, and through faith you will be able to lift your chin up high.

Look only to the Lord. Even though you may not feel anything, even though you may not touch anything, and even though your future looks like a pitch dark night, do not be afraid. You are living by revelational knowledge. You are living with new thoughts, the thoughts of God, the thoughts of His Word, the Bible.

Jesus Christ is the same yesterday, today and forever. Jehovah God never changes, and the Word of God never falls on the ground without being fulfilled.

We cannot live by bread alone, but by the Word of God. We are the righteous children of God, and we must live by faith. In Jesus Christ there is no difference, whether one is black or white, yellow or red, for we all belong to one race, the race of Jesus Christ. And we live by His thinking. So renew your mind and retrain your thought life.

Think big. Have big objectives. You have only one life to live, so do not grovel around in the dust, living with a failure consciousness. Your life is precious to the Lord, and you must contribute something to this world. Jesus Christ dwells with glory in every Christian. You have therefore an endless resource in your life.

Christ is as powerful as He was two thousand years ago. You can renew your thinking by engrafting the thoughts of Jesus Christ into your heart, by thinking positively, by thinking in terms of miracles, and by developing a success orientation of victory and abundance consciousness. This provides a foundation from which you can see the Word of God in your mind, renewing it completely. You will then see great miracles occur.

The Law of Thinking-Asking

Ephesians 3:20 reads, "Now unto Him that is able to do exceeding abundantly above all that we ask or think, according to the power that worketh in us." I call this principle the law of thinking-asking. Many people think that they will receive just by asking. The Bible, however, says "ask or think." God gives answers through your thought life, "exceeding abundantly above all that we ask or think."

What do you think? Do you think poverty? Do you think sickness? Do you think impossibility? Do you think negatively? Do you think failure? If you pray this way God has no channel through which to flow.

What is your thinking life like? Have you renewed your thought life? God is going to do exceeding abundantly, according to the renewal of your thinking life.

You must read the Bible. But do not read the Bible for religious pretenses; do not read the Bible to seek out new legalistic rules for living; do not read the Bible for historical purposes. Rather, read the Bible to feed your mind and to renew your thinking life. Fill your thinking with the Word of God. Then God can have a free approach to your life and flow out to do mighty things for the glory of God through you.

6

GOD'S ADDRESS

When we become Christians not only do we need to retrain our thought life through thinking positively, thinking in terms of miracles and developing an orientation to success; we also need to be aware of our source of power and enablement.

The Confusion

In 1958 I went on my first pioneering work in the worst slum area of our city. But I was not equipped or trained for that kind of ministry. In less than three months all my sermons ran out, and after three months I had nothing to preach.

You may easily say that you will go out and tell the story of salvation, but you cannot speak of salvation only, day in and day out. To make one sermon I spent one entire week going from Genesis to Revelation, and I had the summaries of all the books of the Bible, but I had not one sermon. I almost felt that I was not called into the ministry because I could not make any more sermons.

The poor people in my area were not too concerned about heaven or hell; they lived from hand to mouth each day, and their concern was with everyday survival.

They had no time to think of their future. Wherever I went they asked me to help them with rice, or clothes, or some money to build a shack to live under. But I was no better off than they, as I, too, was living under a shack, going without food, and owning only one suit. So I had nothing to give to them.

I was in a discouraging situation, and though I knew that God had all resources, in those days I did not know how to touch the Lord and tap those resources. There were times I felt that I was near to the Lord, and I felt I was touching Him; but the next day it seemed I was completely out of touch.

So many times I was confused and wondered whether I was really living in the Holy Spirit. Many a time I would say, "Oh, Lord, I know that I am in Jesus Christ." But after having a difficut day, in the evening when I tried to pray I would find that I was completely out of touch with Him. So I would say, "Father, I am confused. I am so much in and out of Thy Person that I do not know how to always keep You by my side." Then my struggle to find the permanent presence of God began.

Oriental people in particular require the address and location of the god they worship. Most Oriental people grow up under the influence of heathen worship, and they need the location or address of their god in order to go and worship it. When I needed my god in heathenism, I would go to a temple and kneel down before an idol, so I could address myself to him directly. In heathenism one has the address of his or her god or gods.

But when I came to Christianity I could not locate the address of our God. That was always great trouble to my heart. In the Lord's prayer we say, "Heavenly Father." I would reason, "Where is heaven?" Well, since the earth is round, for the people living on top, heaven is above them; but for those people who are living on the bottom, heaven is below."

So whenever 'Heavenly Father' was mentioned, I was confused. "Father, where are you?" I would ask. "Are you there? Here? Where? Father, please give me your address!"

Therefore, when Orientals come to Christianity they have a real struggle, because they cannot find the address of God. Many would come to me and ask, "Pastor Cho, give us at least some picture, or even an image, to address to. You ask us to believe in God, but where is He?"

In the first portion of my ministry I would reply to them, "Just speak to the Heavenly Father. I don't know His address or location. Sometimes He comes to me, and other times He doesn't."

I would often cry to Him, for I could not keep on preaching like that. I needed to have a definite address. So I started seeking the address of our God.

In my imagination I went to Adam and I said, "Mr. Adam, I am sure that you are our forefather. I know that you know the address. Please tell me the address of our Heavenly Father."

Then he would very gladly tell me, saying, "Well, He dwelleth in the Garden of Eden. If you go there you will find the location of the Father."

"When you fell from grace," I asked, "you were removed from the Garden of Eden. What is the address of it?"

Adam replied, "Well, I guess I don't know."

I then decided in my imagination to visit Abraham. I was discouraged but I came to Abraham and said, "Mr. Abraham, you are a father of faith, and you met God often. Will you please tell me the address of our Father?"

Abraham replied, "Well, whenever I needed God I put up an altar and I killed an animal, and I waited upon Him. Sometimes He would meet me, and other times He wouldn't. So I don't know His address."

Then I left Abraham and came to Moses and said, "Mr. Moses, surely you know the address of God the Father. You had His presence continually."

"Of course I know Him," Moses replied. "He was in the tabernacle built in the wilderness. During the day He was in the pillar of cloud, and in the night He was in the pillar of fire. You go there and you will meet God. God's address is there."

"But," I said, "when the Israelites came into the land of Canaan, the tabernacle of the wilderness disappeared. Where is the tabernacle of the wilderness?"

"I don't know now," Moses answered.

Again discouraged, I came to King Solomon. I said, "King Solomon, you built a magnificent temple with colorful granite stones. Do you know God's address now?"

"Of course. God dwells in the wonderful temple of Solomon," he told me. "When a curse or sickness spread in my country, the people would pray to the God who dwelled in the temple, and God would listen to them and answer their prayers."

"Where is the temple?" I asked. "That temple was destroyed six hundred years before Christ by the Babylonians. We don't have the address of that temple now."

"Well, I'm sorry," Solomon returned. "That temple was destroyed, and now I don't know the address."

Then I went to John the Baptist. I said, "Mr. John the Baptist, surely you know the address of God."

"Yes," John replied. "Look at the Lamb of God who carried away the sins of the world, Jesus Christ. He is the address of our God."

So in my journey to find the address of God I came to Jesus. Surely in Jesus I would find God. Through Jesus God spoke, and through the one and only Son He performed miracles. Wherever Jesus dwelt, there God also dwelt.

I rejoiced in my heart to find the address of God. Yet still a great question came into my heart. Jesus died, was resurrected and ascended into heaven; so where is the address of Jesus Christ? Once again then, I came all the way back to the starting point. I asked, "Jesus, where are you? I don't know your address and I can't tell my people your location."

The Solution

Then the answer came. Jesus said, "I died and I am resurrected. I have sent the Holy Spirit to each and every one of my followers. I told you that I would never leave you as an orphan. I told you that I would pray to the Father and He would send the Holy Spirit to you, and in that day you would know that I am in the Father, the Father in me, I in you, and you in me."

Gradually I began to see that through the Holy

Spirit, God the Father and God the Son dwelt right in me. I read in II Corinthians that God sealed us and sent His Holy Spirit right into our own hearts. I found the address of God. I found that His address is *my* address.

I then went out to my Christians and began to boldly preach to them, "We can find the location of God. I have now found His address. His address is my address, and He dwelleth in me with all power and authority. Through the Holy Spirit God the Father and God the Son dwelleth in me, and He goes with me where I go.

"He also dwells within you, and His address is your address. If you stay in your home, He is there; if you go to your place of business, He is there; if you work in the kitchen, He is there. God dwelleth within you, and His resources are found in you.

"Brethren," I would continue on, "silver and gold have I none. Food, rice and clothes have I none, but I have something to give you. God dwells within you. Those of you who have not, come to Jesus Christ, receive Him as your personal Savior; and the Creator of heaven and earth, with all of His resources, is going to dwell within your heart. He is going to supply your every need." Hearing this message they began to develop their faith.

That was the starting point of my ministry, and the

foundation stone of my preaching life. Up until that time I was trying to catch God from this place to that. When famous evangelists would come, I would rush to hear them in order to catch God. Sometimes I would go to a mountain to pray, sometimes to a valley. I searched everywhere to find God, but after finding this truth I wandered no more. I had found the address and the location of God.

I say to my people, "God is not a million miles away; He is not God of two thousand years ago; He is not just God of the future. Your God dwelleth in you with all His resources, power and authority; His address is in you. So you can talk and pray to Him everyday, and at any time. You can touch Him and tap His resources through prayer and faith. When you cry aloud, God listens. When you speak softly, God listens. When you meditate, God still hears, for He dwells within you, and He can supply all your needs."

After the Korean war, when the missionaries came out to work for the Lord, I used to attend executive committee meetings. There most of the Korean ministers would introduce all kinds of different projects, such as the construction of churches or the operation of the Bible colleges, and among themselves, discuss the various ways they could bring solution. But when the problem of finance came up, immediately they would say, "Let a missionary come and take over." They used the missionary just as financier.

I became aggravated in my heart and would ask, "Why do you always turn to the missionaries?"

They would reply "God only supplies through the missionary, not through us."

However, from the time I graduated from Bible school I was determined to make God my absolute resource. I found that my God was dwelling in my heart, with all the needed resources. I discovered how to tap God's resources, and all through these twenty years of ministry I have never depended upon any other.

I have crossed over the Pacific Ocean more than forty times to minister in foreign countries, and I have never asked for a penny from a single church. I would express appreciation for the sending of missionaries to Korea, but I have never asked for financial help from foreign churches.

I depended upon God every time; through thick and thin He has supplied all my needs: building the church, sending out missionaries from my church to other countries, and building the Bible college.

Right now we are in the process of building our new Korean Assemblies of God Bible College, and we are giving half a million dollars from my church. God indeed supplies all our needs.

The Challenge

I want to impress upon your heart the fact that you have the resources you need within you right now— not tomorrow, not yesterday, but right now; you have all of God dwelling within you. God is not there sleeping. God never came just to put up a tent and enjoy a vacation. God is there to work out your salvation. And God never works without coming through your thinking, without coming through your vision, without coming through your faith. You are the channel.

You can say, "Oh God, please work mysteriously in the universe and do all things." God will reply, "No! I am dwelling within you. I will never come out to the world with power, without coming through your life."

You are the channel. You have all the responsibility. If you do not develop your way of believing to cooperate with God, God will be limited. God is as large as you allow Him to be; He is also as small as you confine Him to be.

When sinners come to the Lord, broken and unhappy, I teach them first that God is dwelling within them and that they have all resource in Jesus Christ. Then I re-educate them to develop their hearts for cooperation with God. One by one, without exception, they strike out with new faith and lead a miraculous, victorious life.

If these people were all poverty-stricken and filled with failure, how is it that they have given more than twenty million dollars to their church from 1969 to 1977? Every year we carry out projects costing from one and a half to two million dollars. These members can give because they have been enriched, and they are tremendous successes because they know how to tap the Resource. But first they must be cleansed of sins of the flesh.

Most people are at war with four sins of the flesh that should be conquered before the Christian can work actively with God. Without ridding themselves of these sins their channels will be so clogged that God would have no opportunity to flow through them. These are four things I have discovered as a result of twenty years of counseling with people.

The Sin of Hatred

People suffer because of hatred, the first sin we will discuss. If you keep hatred in your heart you can never have God flowing through you. But that hatred, that unforgiving spirit, will be the number one enemy to your faith life. In Matthew 6:14–15, Christ Jesus pointed this out, "For if ye forgive men their trespasses, your heavenly Father will also forgive you: But if ye forgive not men their trespasses, neither will your Father forgive your trespasses."

Usually because I am so tired I do not meet anyone after preaching the fourth multiple Sunday morning service. But if someone does come to my door he must first come through my secretaries, who carefully screen people. If someone does successfully reach my door, then he must be in great need.

One day, after the fourth service a man knocked on the door of my office.

I opened the door and this man came into the room. I thought he might be drunk, for he walked with such a staggering step. He sat down and pulled something from his pocket. It was a sharp dagger, and I was frightened. I thought, "What are these girls doing letting him in here? Here he is with a dagger, and they let him in."

I was really frightened, and as he handled the dagger I prepared to defend myself. I then said, "Don't use that knife. Tell me why you came in here."

He replied, "Sir, I'm going to commit suicide. But first I'm going to kill my wife, my father-in-law, my mother-in-law and everybody around me. My friend advised me to come and attend one of your services before I do all these things, so I came and attended the fourth service. I listened intently but I couldn't understand one word, because you were speaking with such a strong Southern provincial accent. I couldn't understand your accent, and I couldn't catch any of your words. So after listening to you, I am going to go and carry out all of my plans.

"I am a dying man. I have tuberculosis, and I am constantly coughing. I am dying."

"Calm down," I urged him. "Sit here and tell me your story."

"Well," he replied, "during the last stage of the Vietnamese War I went out as a technician and bulldozer driver. I worked all through the front lines making bunkers and roads, risking my life in order to make more money. I sent all the money to my wife, and when the war was over I had scarcely enough to come out of Vietnam.

"I sent a telegram from Hong Kong to my wife, and when I arrived at Seoul Airport I was expecting to see her with our children; but when I got there I couldn't find even a shadow of them. I thought that perhaps they hadn't received my telegram, but when I rushed home I found strangers living there.

"I found out that my wife had run away with a young man. She had left me, taking all of my savings, and was running away with another man, and was living in another part of town. I went to her and begged her to come back to me; but she was adamant, determined not to return.

"I went to my wife's father and mother's home and protested. They gave me $40 and then chased me out of their house. In less than a week I had a burning hatred in my heart, and I began to vomit blood. Now tuberculosis is fast eating me away, and there is no hope for me. I am going to destroy them, every one of them, and then I am going to kill myself."

"Sir," I told him, "this is not the way to carry out your revenge. The best way to get yourself healed is to find a new job, make a better and more beautiful home, and show yourself off to them. In this way you can really carry out your revenge; but if you kill all of them and then kill yourself, it would not bring any satisfaction."

"I hate them," he cried.

"So long as you hate them you are going to destroy yourself," I said. "When you hate you destroy yourself more than you do others.

"Why don't you try Jesus?" I asked. "When Jesus comes into your heart all the power of God comes and dwells within you. The power of God will flow through you. God will touch you, heal you, and restore your life. You can reconstruct your life, and that would be real revenge against your enemies."

I sent him to Prayer Mountain, where he accepted
Jesus Christ as his personal Saviour. But still he could
not totally forgive his wife. So I asked him to bless his
wife, "The best way of forgiving your wife is to bless
her: bless her spirit, soul, body and life. Pray to God
that He will open the door of heaven with blessings for
her."

"I can't bless her!" he exclaimed. "I will not curse
her, but I cannot bless her."

I answered, "If you don't bless her, you are not
going to be healed. When you bless, the blessings
start from you and go out; you are going to be more
blessed by your words of blessing than she is. In Korea
there is an old saying, "If you want to smear the face of
others with mire, you will have to smear your hand
first.' So if you curse your wife, the curse will flow out
of your mouth first, and you will be cursed first. But if
you bless your wife, the word of blessing bubbles
up from your heart, going through your mouth, and
you become blessed first. So go ahead and bless her."

He sat down and began to bless her, at first while
grinding his teeth. He prayed, "Oh God, I bless...my
wife. Bless...her. And...give her salvation. Oh God,
give her...a blessing."

He kept on blessing her, and in less than a month he
was completely healed from tuberculosis and a changed

person. The power of God began flowing out of him, and his face shone.

When I met him after a month he excitedly said, "Oh, Pastor Cho, I rejoice in the Lord! I praise God that now I really appreciate my wife, for it was because she left me that I found Jesus. I pray for her every day. I have renewed my license as a bulldozer driver. I have a new job, I'm making a new home, and I'm waiting for my wife to come back."

This man was praising the Lord. He was reconstructing his life through the power of God which had begun to flow out of him. He was healed in spirit and body.

Without getting rid of your hatred you cannot really get in touch with the Lord. When you go out in the ministry you must help people to realize this.

One day a schoolteacher came to see me. A principal of a school, she was suffering from arthritis. She had gone to every hospital but could not be cured. I laid hands on her, prayed, rebuked, shouted – I did everything I could, but God did not touch her.

Many people had been healed in the church, but in spite of everything, she was not healed. Eventually I began to feel like giving up. But one day the Holy Spirit said, "Don't shout, pray and rebuke. I can't flow out of her because she hates her former husband."

I knew that she had been divorced ten years ago,

but as she was sitting there I said, "Sister, please divorce your husband."

She looked at me and said, "Pastor, what do you mean, divorce my husband? I divorced him more than ten years ago."

"No, you didn't," I replied.

"Oh yes, I did!" she insisted.

"Yes," I replied, "of course you did—legally. But mentally you have never divorced him. Every morning you curse him. Every day you curse and hate him; in your imagination you have never divorced your husband. In your mind you are still living with him, and that hatred is destroying you and drying up your bones. Because of this your arthritis is incurable. No doctor could cure you."

She retorted, "Oh, but he did such harm. When I married him he never got a job. He used all my income. He messed up my life, then he left me to go with another woman. How could I love him?"

I replied, "Whether you love him or not is your business; but if you don't love him you are going to die from arthritis. The arthritis is going to be healed only by the power of God. The power of God will never fall down from the sky like a meteor and touch and heal you.

"No!" I continued, "God is dwelling within you, and He is going to well up from within you and heal you. But you hinder the flow of God's power with your hatred. Please begin to bless your husband. Bless your enemy and do good to him. Then you will grow to love him and create a channel through which God's Holy Spirit is going to flow and touch you."

She had the same struggle as the man with tuberculosis. Crying she said, "I can't love him. Pastor, please forgive me. I will not hate him, but I will not love him."

"You can't stop hating him if you don't positively love him," I replied. "Look at your husband in your imagination; touch him and tell him that you love him, and bless him."

Once again she struggled, so I led a prayer for her. She cried, gritting her teeth. But eventually she began to feel love for him, and praying she asked God to bless and save him and give every good thing to him. God's power started flowing in her, and she was touched. In less than three months she was delivered from her arthritis.

Yes, God is dwelling within you. But if you do not rid yourself of that archenemy hate, then God's power cannot flow through you.

The Sin of Fear

Many people live under fear. It is our responsibility as Christians to help people rid themselves of this fear, the second sin in this group of four.

Once I had tuberculosis. I had tuberculosis because I was constantly living under the fear of tuberculosis. When I was a student in junior high school, one of the classes I went to had bottles of alcohol filled with bones and intestines. The sight of these bottles filled with bones and intestines frightened me.

One morning the biology teacher was teaching on the subject of tuberculosis. In those days there were no miracle drugs, and the teacher said if you ever had tuberculosis you would be dissipated, your insides looking like these bottles, the rest of your life.

He told of the dangers of tuberculosis, and at the close said, "There are people who are born with a tendency to have tuberculosis. Men with narrow shoulders and long necks seem more apt to catch tuberculosis."

All the students began to stretch their necks out like cranes, and in looking around I saw that I had the longest neck in my classroom. Right away I knew that I would get tuberculosis. Fear struck me; when I got back to my room, I stood before the mirror, looking at my neck all afternoon. Fear came into my heart, and every moment I lived under the grinding fear of tuberculosis.

When I turned 18 years old I did have tuberculosis. Like attracts like, and like produces like. If you have fear, the devil has an open channel through which to come and strike you; fear is negative faith. So, as I feared tuberculosis, I contracted tuberculosis, and as I vomited blood I said to myself, "Yes, this is exactly as I expected."

I read in a Korean medical journal that some doctors claim that many Korean people die habitually. I thought to myself, "How can people die from habit?" Then I read the article.

These non-Christian doctors wrote how strong a role fear plays in our lives. For example, a man's grandfather died from high blood pressure in his fifties. His son, when in his fifties, also died of a stroke. Now the grandson lives in fear of dying of a stroke.

When he reaches his fifties the moment he feels a dizziness in his head he thinks, "Oh, a stroke is coming. I am ready." If he feels something in his chest he waits momentarily for a stroke, each day living with this fear and expectancy. The fear creates this situation in his body, and soon he does die of a stroke.

Many women die because of the fear of cancer. One woman might say, "Well, my aunt died of cancer, and my mother died of cancer, so I'll probably die of cancer, too."

When she reaches an age similar to that of her aunt and mother at their deaths, she will feel any type of pain and say, "Oh, this is cancer. It certainly is coming now." Everyday she will wait, saying to herself that she is going to have cancer, repeating this thought over and over. It is in this way that the doctors said people were dying from habit. If a person has a specific fear, then the power of destruction begins to flow.

In 1969 when God asked me to move from my second church, I had 10,000 members with 12,000 regularly attending. I was happy, feeling good and satisfied. I had a good home, a wonderful wife, children, a beautiful car and even a chauffeur. I responded, "God, I am going to stay at this church until my black hair turns white."

But one day while I was praying in my office, the Holy Spirit came, "Cho, your time is up here. You must be ready to move."

"Oh, Lord," I said. "Move? I already pioneered one church, and this is my second pioneer work. Do you want me to pioneer again? Why should I pioneer constantly? You are choosing the wrong person. Go to someone else," and I started arguing with God.

No one, however, should argue with God, for He is always right. Eventually God persuaded me, saying, "You go out and build a church which will seat 10,000, a church that will send out at least 500 missionaries."

"Father," I replied, "I can't do that. I'm scared to

death of building a church like that."

But God said, "No, I've told you to go. Now go."

I calculated roughly with a contractor about costs. He told me that we needed two-and-a-half million dollars to build that size a church, another half million to purchase the land, and an additional two-and-one-half million to build an adjacent apartment complex. So I would need five-and-one-half million dollars.

The contractor asked me how much money I had. I told him I had $2,500. He looked blankly at me, shook his head, and did not even comment.

Then I went to a meeting of our church's elders and told them the plan. One elder said, "Pastor, how much money are you going to raise in America?"

"Not a penny," I answered.

Another elder asked, "How much money can you borrow from the American Bank?"

"Not one penny," I replied.

They said, "You are a good, genuine minister, but you're no businessman. You can't build a church and apartment house like that."

Then I called the 600 deacons together. And I told them the plan, but they immediately began to act like scared rabbits, as if I were levying a high tax on their lives.

I became discouraged. Full of fear, I came to

the Lord, "Lord, you heard every word the elders and deacons said. They were all in agreement, so you've got to think this over again."

Then the Spirit spoke strongly in my heart, "Son, when did I ask you to go and talk with the elders and deacons?"

"Am I not supposed to?" I asked.

The Spirit answered, "I commanded you to build the church, not to discuss it. That's my command."

I lifted myself up and said, "Yes, if it's your command, then I will do it."

I went to City Hall and on credit bought four acres of expensive land located near Congress Hall, one of the choicest pieces of land in Korea. Then I went to the contractor and made a contract to build that church and apartment house complex, also on credit. I thought to myself, "They will build the church easily. I will trust God and see."

After the ground breaking service I went out to look around. I thought they would just dig a few yards down and put up the building. But there they were, digging as if they had to develop a lake, with dozens of bulldozers digging the earth.

I became crazy with fear. I asked, "Father, do you see how they're digging? And I have to pay for all this? Oh, I can't," and I was frozen with fear. My knees trembled, and in my imagination I saw myself carried away in a prison van. I knelt down and prayed, "Oh God, what can I do? Where can I stand? Where are you? I know that you are the total Resource, and I put my trust in You."

When I prayed I could envision God's workings and I no longer had any fear; but when I opened my eyes and looked at the situation, again I became fearful. So for the duration of the construction I lived with my eyes closed more than I lived with my eyes open.

The same principle holds true in many situations. If you look at your circumstances with your physical eyes and live by your senses, satan will destroy you with fear. But if you close your eyes and look to God, then you can believe.

There are two different kinds of knowledge–sensual knowledge and revelational knowledge. We should live by the revelational knowledge found in Genesis to Revelation, not by our sensual knowledge.

We should instruct people to give up their fear of the environment and of their circumstances. If they do not, they cannot develop their faith nor can God flow through them. Ask them to surrender their fears to the Lord, and teach them to put their faith only in the Word of God.

The Sin of Inferiority

Many people live with inferiority complexes, and are constantly frustrated; this feeling of inferiority is the third problem area I will discuss.

If people feel that they are inferior because they live in a slum area, you cannot pull them out. Perhaps they failed in their businesses and have resigned themselves to being a failure. But so long as they have this attitude, you cannot help them. You must ask each to surrender his inferiority complex, and let himself be reconstructed by the love of God.

One day an older brother of elementary school age killed his younger brother with a knife. This became a sensational news topic. It was found that the parents had loved the younger son very much, constantly praising him in the presence of his older brother; eventually the older brother began to feel inferior. One day when his parents were out, his younger brother came back from school, and the elder brother killed him. An inferiority complex is very destructive.

I once suffered with an inferiority complex. After two years in my first pioneer work, my church was progressively growing; but it was a loud church, a true Pentecostal church. People were filled with the Holy Spirit and many were healed. One day the Executive

Committee of my denonination called me. At that time they stood somewhere between the expressive Pentecostal and the staid Presbyterian.

They questioned me, "Are you really praying for the sick and getting the people to shout and speak in other tongues in your services?"

"Yes," I replied.

"You are a fanatic," they asserted.

"I am not a fanatic. I am doing everything according to biblical teaching," I defended.

After discussing this, they took my ministerial license and sent me out. I was chased out of my own denomination. Afterwards missionary John Hurston came and took me back.

When I was cast out I was struck with feelings of inferiority. That inferiority complex brought about a feeling of destruction in me, and I had a difficult time struggling out of that situation.

At the time the members of the Executive Committee put me out, however, they did not realize I was one day to be General Superintendent of that same denomination. That is a post I held until recently. When I first came to that responsibility, we had only 2,000 members. By applying the laws of faith and teaching them to the pastors, we experienced rapid growth. By the time I resigned from that position our census revealed that the denomination had a total of 300 churches with more than 200,000 members.

We must deal with those who feel that they are unable to conquer life. We must pull them out of their depression and pessimism, build them up in the love of Jesus Christ and impart faith to them, telling them that nothing is impossible to the person who believes. We must heal them and train them, and by and by they are going to pull out of their inferiority feelings.

One Sunday morning as I was preaching at the second worship service I saw a man I knew was mentally sick, brought in with his hands and feet bound. That particular day we were making pledges for the fifth stage of our building plans. Many people were filling in pledge cards; when a pledge card came to this man, he wrote in $100 with his bound hand.

His wife laughed when the deacon came to take the pledge card. "Don't believe him," she said. "He's crazy."

But after the service when I met him, he was completely healed by the power of the Holy Spirit, having returned again to his right mind. He had been deeply suffering from an inferiority complex. He explained, "I had a fertilizer factory, and I failed and went heavily into debt. I worried so much I lost my mind. Then they took me to an institution and gave me all kinds of electric shock treatments; but I couldn't be cured.

"But as I was sitting there listening to your words, I suddenly came out of my state of sickness and recognized reality. I've lost my friends, my prestige, and my credit. I have a mountain of debts. I can do nothing. I am nothing."

"You are something," I told him. "You are not inferior. You came to Jesus, and now all of the power of Christ and all His resources dwell within you. You are going to be used by God. You are not inferior, for you are God's man. Stand victoriously. You have all power and resources dwelling within you, just waiting to be tapped."

"What kind of job am I going to have?" he questioned me.

"I don't know," I replied, "but keep on reading the Bible, and pray."

One day he returned, filled with excitement. "Pastor, I read the verse of Scripture that says we are the salt of the world. How about my going into the retail business of selling salt?"

"If you believe in it," I said, "go right ahead. Do it!"

So he went out, selling salt on a small scale. He paid tithes, paid his pledge and all the time was rejoicing in the Lord. God began to bless him, and his salt business grew and grew. Eventually he built a large storehouse right beside the river, where he placed $50,000 worth of salt.

But one summer night it rained heavily, and in the morning when I got up all the area had completely flooded. His storehouse also was flooded, and I was struck with fear. That afternoon when the rain stopped, I rushed out to his store.

Other articles and materials can still be found after a flood, but salt has a great friendship with water. When I entered the storehouse there was no salt left. The man, now an elder in the church, was sitting in the middle of his warehouse, singing and praising God. I walked in, trying to discern whether or not he was in his right mind. I went up to him and asked, "Are you okay, or are you crazy?"

"Pastor, I'm the real me," he smiled. "I'm not crazy. Don't worry. I've lost everything. God took it away; but as you always told me, I have all the resources here. Water could take away my salt, but water can't take away the total resources of the presence of God dwelling within me. I can tap those resources again and again by prayer and faith. You wait. Give me time. I'll rebuild my business again."

He was not suffering from an inferiority complex then. He was full of confidence. Now he is a multi-millionaire through his salt business. He also went into watch production and has his own company. He has accompanied me to Los Angeles, Vancouver and New York; he recently went tŏ Europe.

His is just one example of how we can help rid people of their feelings of inferiority by stressing that they have all God's resources at their disposal to tap.

The Sin of Guilt

Many people also suffer from feelings of guilt, the fourth problem that needs to be overcome before the Christian can work actively with God; for as long as someone suffers from guilt, God can never flow through him. We need to help people rid themselves of their guilt feelings; we need to stress to them that when you feel that you are unworthy and full of guilt, then you can simply come to the Lord, and He will cleanse you.

One day I was in my office and a beautiful couple walked in. The man was quite a handsome person, and his wife very lovely. But even though this lovely wife was in her early thirties, she was emaciated, so emaciated she could hardly open her eyes.

Her husband said, "Pastor, my wife is dying. I've tried everything—psychology, psychiatry, and all the internal and external medicine imaginable. I'm a rich man. I've spent thousands and thousands of dollars on her, but the doctors could do nothing. Now they've

given up hope. I have heard that you have really helped
many people, and they have been healed."

I told him that this was true, and I looked at her,
searching for the discernment and wisdom she needed
in this situation. Silently I prayed, "Lord, she has come
here. Now what can I do?"

Right away God's still, small voice spoke, "She is
suffering from a psychosomatic sickness. This is not an
organic sickness; this is a mental sickness."

I asked her husband to leave the room and said,
"Lady, do you want to live? You need to live for your
husband's sake, at least. If you were going to die you
should have done so before, because now you have three
children. If you die now, leaving your children with
your husband, you'll really mess up his life. So sink or
swim, you've got to live for your husband and your
children."

"I would like to live," she told me.

"Then I can help you only on one condition. You
must open up your past life," I answered.

She straightened up and with anger glaring in her
eyes said, "Am I in a police station? Are you a dictator
here? Why do you ask this? This is not an interrogation,
and I don't have to open up my past."

"I can't help you, then," I replied. "If you persist
like this, I am going to ask God to directly reveal the

problem areas of your past."

She was frightened, and taking out a handkerchief from her purse she began to cry. After a long sigh she said, "Sir, I will open up my past life. But I don't think this is the trouble."

"Yes, it is," I said. "This is the cause of your problem."

"My parents died when I was young, and I was practically raised in my elder sister's house. My sister was like a mother to me, and my brother-in-law like a father. They took care of me wonderfully, and I lived with them while attending junior high school, high school, and college.

"When I was in my third year of college my elder sister went into the hospital to give birth to her last child. During that time I took care of the home and children. Without recognizing what was happening, my brother-in-law and I fell in love with each other.

"I don't know what happened to me, but we fell into an immoral relationship; then guilt really struck into my heart. From that moment on I was dying from guilt. But my brother-in-law would keep calling me from his office, and we would constantly meet at motels, hotels and resort areas.

"I went to the hospital and had several abortions, and even then I could not refuse the requests of my brother-in-law. I was scared to death of letting my sister know, so my brother-in-law continually intimidated me; I was slowly being destroyed.

"When I graduated from college I determined that I would marry the first man who proposed to me. I found a job, and the young man who is now my husband asked me to marry him, with no questions asked about my past; I accepted, just so I could get away from my brother-in-law. I married him, and in time he became quite prosperous. He resigned from his former work and began his own business. Now he is well off. We have a good home, money—everything.

"But since that time with my brother-in-law, I have been suffering from these strong feelings of guilt. Whenever my husband makes love to me I feel like a prostitute, for I have no right to receive his love; inside I am torn and crying. My children are like angels, and they come and hug me, saying, "Mama!" And I hate myself. I know that I am a prostitute. I am not worthy to receive this kind of love from my children. I don't like to look at my face in the mirror. That is the reason I can't attire myself in the proper way. I've lost my taste for food and have no happiness or joy in my heart."

"You must forgive yourself," I told her. "I have good news for you. Jesus Christ came and died for you and your sins on the cross."

"Not even Jesus can forgive my sins," she cried. "My sins are too great and too deep to be forgiven. I've done everything. Everyone else can be forgiven, but not me! I deceived my sister, and I can't confess what I've done to her. That would mean breaking up her whole life."

Silently I wondered, "Oh Lord, how can I help her now? You've got to help me." Then I listened for a still, small voice within my heart and suddenly got an idea.

"Sister, close your eyes," I instructed her, also doing the same thing myself. "Let's go to a very silent and beautiful lake. Now you and I are sitting beside the lake, and there are many pebbles. In my hand I hold a very small pebble. You please pick up a big rock. Let's throw this pebble and this rock into the lake.

"First it's my turn. I take hold of the pebble and cast it in. Did you hear the sound it made? A ripple. Where is my pebble now?"

She answered, "Well, it went down to the bottom of the lake."

"Right," I replied. "Now it's your turn. Cast your rock in. Yes, you cast it in...okay, now that you've cast it in, did it make a light noise?"

"No," she asserted, "it made a big sound, and a large ripple."

"But where is your rock?" I asked.

"Down at the bottom," she replied.

"Well, it seems that both my small pebble and your big rock went to the bottom when they were thrown. The only difference was the sound and ripple. Mine made a plop, yours made a boom. Mine made a small ripple, yours a large ripple. People go to hell with small sins just as well as big sins, for they are without Jesus Christ. And what is the difference? Sound and its influence on society. Everyone needs the forgiveness of Jesus Christ. The blood of Jesus cures all sins, big and little."

This touched her soul, and she woke to the truth. "Does that mean that my sins could be forgiven by God?"

"Of course," I replied.

She slumped in her chair and began to cry, shivering. I tried to encourage and cheer her, but she continued to cry and cry. Then I laid my hand on her and led her in the sinner's prayer.

Afterwards, when she lifted her face, I saw her eyes shining like the stars, and glory began to shine from her face. She stood up and exclaimed, "Pastor, I'm saved! All my burdens are lifted!"

I began to sing, and she began to dance. Before this time she had never danced for joy before the Lord, but this day she jumped and danced, making quite a bit of noise. Her husband heard the noise and rushed into the office. When she saw him she rushed to him and hugged his neck. She had never done that before, and her husband was unbelieving.

He asked, "What have you done to her?"

"God has performed a miracle!" I answered joyfully.

"You must give your whole heart to the Lord," I said, turning to his wife. "The Lord has done great things for you." She soon was rid entirely from her guilt; then the power of God welled up in her, and she was healed completely.

That couple now attend my church, and whenever I look at the face of that lady, I cannot help thinking of the love of Jesus Christ. Now she has no sickness and is completely healed; when she let go of her clogging sin of guilt, the power of God flowed forth.

Brothers and sisters in Christ, right now you have all God's power dwelling within you. You can tap that power for your tuition, your clothes, your books, your health, your business, everything! When you go out to preach the gospel you are not preaching a vague objective, a theory, philosophy, or human religion. You are actually teaching people how to tap endless resources. You are giving them Jesus, and through Jesus God comes and dwells within our hearts.